Final
SCORE!

DAN FARR

Final SCORE!

ON THE TEE

TATE PUBLISHING
AND ENTERPRISES, LLC

This book is designed to provide accurate and authoritative information with regard to the subject matter covered. This information is given with the understanding that neither the author nor Tate Publishing, LLC is engaged in rendering legal, professional advice. Since the details of your situation are fact dependent, you should additionally seek the services of a competent professional.

The opinions expressed by the author are not necessarily those of Tate Publishing, LLC.

Published by Tate Publishing & Enterprises, LLC
127 E. Trade Center Terrace | Mustang, Oklahoma 73064 USA
1.888.361.9473 | www.tatepublishing.com

Tate Publishing is committed to excellence in the publishing industry. The company reflects the philosophy established by the founders, based on Psalm 68:11,
"The Lord gave the word and great was the company of those who published it."

Book design copyright © 2015 by Tate Publishing, LLC. All rights reserved.
Cover design by Gian Philipp Rufin
Interior design by Caypeeline Casas

Published in the United States of America

ISBN: 978-1-68118-839-3
1. Self-Help / Motivational & Inspirational
2. Sports & Recreation / Golf
15.03.13

To my best friend and wonderful wife, Becca,
and to our daughters, Allison and Jillian.

In memory of my father, Lester E. Farr Sr.;
my mother, Allene Farr;
and my father-in-law, Damon Ray.

CONTENTS

Do you know a young person (or an adult) who is crazy about sports but you can't seem to get through to them about their need for Christ? I was once that person, but God used sports to get me, at the age of forty-eight, to break the barrier and see what Christ had done on the cross for me. This book is designed to help you break through that barrier.

Through this collection of devotions and short stories, I have attempted to combine my knowledge of sports, my growing knowledge of the Bible, and everyday experiences to connect the reader to the gospel in a fresh new way. Hopefully one of these stories will reach a young man or young woman for Christ who otherwise might have never known him.

Everyone needs to understand that it is very cool to know Jesus and for him to know us. Jesus taught the people two thousand years ago using ordinary stories about farming, water, marriage, and everyday life, which are called parables. If Jesus wrote parables today, undoubtedly, he would toss in a few sports stories since so many people today are passionate about sports. Apostle Paul shared with the

Corinthians in 1 Corinthians 9:22, "Whatever a person is like, I try to find common ground with him, so that he will let me tell him about Christ, and let Christ save him." My hope and prayer is to share these sports-related parables in a way that the light bulb will come on for you to enable you to look at the cross as you never have before and allow God to change you and disciple you. To God be all the glory that might result from this book.

TESTIMONY

I am honored and privileged to share my testimony with you. On a Sunday morning in the late 1960s, in a small Methodist church in Middle Georgia, I could have received Christ. I was drawn to Jesus Christ by the Holy Spirit during a message by a lay speaker, but I was afraid of what people would say if I went to the altar. I escaped into the warm sunshine and convinced myself that I would have enough nerve to accept Christ the following Sunday. But I went back into the wilderness for thirty-five years. I did not attend church when I moved to Atlanta, but I met my future wife, Becca, through the sports ministry at Peachtree Presbyterian Church. We married the following year and were later blessed with two beautiful daughters, Allison and Jillian. We visited Mt. Zion UMC in East Cobb, which had a new gym. Two years later, I started a basketball program and poured my energy into it for the next twelve years. It was great seeing the program grow and packing the sanctuary on basketball Sunday. But my focus was too much about personal achievement and not enough about helping young people know Christ.

I continued to live a self-centered life and could go for days without communicating with God. But in 2001, I watched the ESPN Classic special about basketball star Pete Maravich, my idol throughout high school, college, and adulthood. My vintage Maravich jersey hung in my closet for twenty-five years. I bought throwback jerseys, books, and videos on eBay. One VHS tape was Pete's testimony, which I watched one Sunday night out of boredom and curiosity. That video was a divine appointment. At the time, I was drifting away from the basketball program and was very unhappy with myself. I was so far from God after many years of living without him. Jesus on the cross? It was just a story until I heard Pete tell how Christ transformed him. I always wanted to be like Pete, but I realized I wasn't because Jesus Christ knew Pete Maravich and Jesus didn't know me. Occasionally, I wondered during sermons, *Am I going to heaven?* Then I would fool myself by falling back on my good works. But I knew that if I died that evening, I would never see Jesus face-to-face. I cried out in my heart that I wanted my life to change. As my former pastor, Steve Lyle, often said, "It's not the words you pray as much as the attitude of your heart."

God has blessed me with many opportunities to share my testimony. At first, I was sure I had it all figured out, but instead, there was so much to learn. God led me to turn that basketball program into our Christ-centered Hoops2Heaven ministry. I eventually allowed him to change me in the workplace when I went through trying times after a merger. An opportunity came to teach high school Sunday school and lead the basketball ministry again, which led to the start of a year-round youth sports ministry at Mt. Zion. Can you see a pattern? Youth sports ministry is my fishing hole. I continue to pray that I can get it right for Christ for our families at Mt. Zion and in our community. God loved me unconditionally, wooed me, and showed me mercy time after time until I repented, which means that I turned from my sinful ways, trusted, and obeyed. Repent, trust, and obey. There is no other way. I'm far from perfect, but God thinks I'm worth it. I was lost and then found and forgiven.

GOLF 01

Give Him the Glory in All that You Do

Philippians 4:13, Colossians 3:17

Whatever you do, in word or deed, do everything
in the name of the Lord Jesus.

—Colossians 3:17 (NASB)

I've always taken pride in my ability as an athlete, having earned ten varsity letters in high school although I graduated when I was only sixteen. I played college golf and still consider myself to be an athlete on the other side of the half-century mark. But in all my athletic competitions, I had never given God the glory during a contest until the Senior Club Championship golf tournament at Alpharetta Country Club in 2006. It wasn't the most competitive tournament, but there were some former college players. The tourney favorites were my good friends, Ralph, a former University of Alabama player who won the overall club championship by eight shots the previous weekend, and Jeff, a former college player from upstate New York and a big left hander, about six feet four inches, who hits it about nine miles.

I never really understood that when I played golf or took part in any activity, I should do it for God's glory. That approach seemed a little farfetched to me. But since I became a Christian in 2003, I certainly have tried to conduct myself with dignity, particularly after my pre-Jesus cursing and club-throwing antics. It just never occurred to me that I should stay connected to God during a four-hour round of golf. During the front nine, I was conscious of God's presence, and I prayed breath prayers to stay calm and take whatever happened in stride. I eagled a par four and took a two-shot lead over Ralph to the back nine. Several times on the back nine, waiting to hit my next shot, I prayed, *God, please allow me to take one shot at a time and stay calm. I praise you for the peace that passes all understanding. I sure could use some of that peace right now!* I didn't pray to win, but I asked God to calm me so that I could perform my next shot well under the growing pressure of hanging onto the lead.

Ralph hung close, and Jeff got back in the tournament with four consecutive birdies. While I felt the pressure from my lead shrinking, I stayed focused and tried not to allow their performances to affect mine. I prayed silently, *God, I will glorify you if I win, and I will glorify you if I lose.* That was a prayer that I heard from Coach Taylor the previous afternoon, when Becca and I saw *Facing the Giants*. The glory that I wanted to give God was not where I finished but how I played. He gave me an inner peace that allowed me to perform well. The defining moment came on the par three seventeenth hole when I put my tee shot six inches from the cup. I tapped it in and won my first stroke-play tournament in twenty-five years. While I was very happy and pleased, I gave the glory to God. I felt that if I had not prayed and spoken to him during the round, I would not have been victorious.

Prayer: Father God, help me realize that you want to be part of every aspect of my life no matter how insignificant I feel it is. Thank you for caring deeply about everything I do. When I do well, may you always receive the glory. In Jesus's name, amen.

The Gospel of the Hole in One

Matthew 7:13, 25:32; John 14:6

Heaven can be entered only
through the narrow gate!

—Matthew 7:13 (TLB)

The biggest thrill for any recreational golfer is to make a hole in one. Many golfers will play golf for a lifetime and never make one. *Golf Digest* once placed the odds of a hole in one at 33,000 to 1. When you consider the factors of the wind, yardage, ball flight, type of ball, hole location, contours of the green, type of club, and the speed of the green, it seems impossible. The hole is only four and a half inches wide, and your tee shot's margin of error is fifty yards in any direction.

Of course, the score for a hole in one is what? One. A one. Let it sink in. I find it interesting that the number 1 is the narrowest number of all the infinite combinations of numbers and integers. In golf, there is 2, 3, 4, 5, 6, the hockey stick 7, and the snowman 8. And there is little, skinny, narrow 1. Incredibly hard to achieve a 1 in golf.

The Bible teaches us about the broad road and the narrow road. Matthew tells us that heaven can only be entered through the narrow gate. Isn't it interesting that from a distance, a narrow gate with high walls on either side is shaped like the number 1.

In life, it's humanly impossible to say no every time to the distractions of the broad road, with its broad gate and all of its sinful trappings. If sin weren't fun, no one would do it, I once heard. We're really comfortable going through the broad gate. Plenty of friends and colleagues are there with us at the broad gate as we bypass the narrow gate. But only the narrow gate leads to the immeasurable joy that can be ours instead of remaining disillusioned and unfulfilled by the temporary interludes of success and happiness of the broad road that can never satisfy us in the end.

Jesus didn't say he is *a* way. He is the Way, one Way. When you hear that somebody made a 1 or if you make a 1, stop and give thanks to the One who took your place on the cross. I'm thankful that I remembered to say, "Thank you, Jesus!" when I made my first hole in one. In June 2008, after thousands of rounds of golf over a forty-plus-year period, I holed an 8-iron from 165 yards on the eleventh hole at the East Course at Alpharetta Athletic Club.

Prayer: Dear Heavenly Father, I am so thankful that you sent the One down from heaven to live among us and save us. And that the One is the one way to heaven. Thank you for Jesus, the One who died for me. In Jesus's name, amen.

GOLF 03

The Truth Sets You Free

John 8:32, 1 John 1:9

Then you will know the Truth,
and the Truth will set you free.

—John 8:32

My daughter Allison played the Atlanta Junior Golf Association (AJGA) summer circuit between her sophomore and junior high school years to gain tournament experience. Golf is a tough-enough sport to learn without the added pressure of competing in tournaments, so she needed experience. Her first few events were difficult adjustments. We were usually up at five and on the road by six to travel to a course in North Georgia. Each time, there was a course that she had never seen, and several girls were quite good, which discouraged her at times. But Allison was very determined to improve.

But in one of her last events, her game came together. She was playing very consistently, and I was enjoying her good play as I walked with the other parents. On the sixth hole, Allison drove her ball into tall, wiry grass, but she played a beautiful escape to the fairway and salvaged her bogey. On the next tee, she drove it long and straight down the fairway, and I saw a smile crease her face in the morning sunlight. Allison chatted with Chelsea, her fellow competitor, as she walked toward her ball for her second shot. As she looked at the ball, I saw her do what I would describe as a double take. She walked toward us, and I could see tears forming in her eyes. Allison walked to the AJGA volunteer with her group and said, "That's not my ball. I must have played the wrong ball out of the rough." I was just heartbroken for her because she was finally playing well in a tournament. Allison was disqualified for playing the wrong ball. The volunteer said, "Allison, it took a lot of courage to come over and tell me." Chelsea tried to console her, and Chelsea's mother said, "Allison, you can watch my money any time!" It was a beautiful compliment and helped ease the sting.

As badly as the DQ hurt, Allison has been able to recall that situation and remember how she acted with integrity. She created a life lesson that carried into her college and professional work careers. She told the truth, and she remains free from wondering if she had made a different choice to keep playing. By the way, the tournament experience paid off as Allison was one of three players to play for her team at region and state the following year. Her Lassiter High School team won the state championship. Allison told her granddad, who won a state title in basketball exactly fifty years before, "We've got another state champ in the family!"

Jesus taught his disciples, "Then you will know the truth, and the truth will set you free." When we fail to follow through with integrity and complete honesty, it will haunt us, but as believers, we are not condemned" (Romans 8:1). If we confess our sins, God is faithful and just and will forgive our sins and cleanse us from all unrighteousness. Once you've confessed, accept God's forgiveness and move forward to the next round. Don't be looking four or five holes back. Forgive and forget is what God does, and so should you. Learn from your experience and move on with your life.

Prayer: Father God, it's so cool the way you give us life lessons to teach us how to behave. Thank you for the presence of the Holy Spirit in our lives that prompts us when the clerk gives us too much money back, when our ball moves in the fairway, when the entire story needs to be told, and when we make decisions with integrity. Forgive me when I fail you, and help me accept your forgiveness and cleanse me anew. In Jesus's name, amen.

GOLF 04

Take Christ into Your Workplace

> Iron sharpens iron, so a man sharpens the
> countenance of his friend.
>
> —Proverbs 27:17

I shared this story with the golfers at the Mark Richt FCA tournament in Athens in May 2007. This picture was taken by Chad, the son of my very good friend Ralph at the Monday Masters practice round. The two golfers are Zach Johnson (L), who would become the 2007 champion just six days later, and Larry Mize (R), the 1987 Masters champion. The significance of this seemingly random photograph is that two Christians are speaking. Larry is probably sharing course knowledge and strategy with Zach, but perhaps they also shared the Word and some faith stories. Zach has no idea that he would become the Masters champ.

After he finished his Sunday round, Zach told the CBS announcer and a national TV audience that he felt that Jesus was with him during the back nine on Sunday. Zach said that he was able to remain calm and that the victory was even more special because it occurred on Easter Sunday. The moral of the story: Zach invited Jesus to become part of his workday. Zach turned to Jesus to bring him peace during a very tense and important time in the midst of his workday. At the end, instead of taking the credit, Zach gave God all the glory. Isn't Zach's example a great golf lesson for us to take Christ into the place where we are working, whether it is at the office or at school? When we have a tough assignment or tough test, Jesus is always there for us.

Prayer: Father God, thank you for always being there for me no matter where I am or what I am doing. Help me shine my light in all situations so I can bring you glory. In Jesus's precious name, amen.

Zach Johnson (L) and Larry Mize (R)
on the putting green before the Masters practice round

GOLF 05

Set Your Face Like Flint

Because the Lord God helps me, I will not be dismayed. Therefore I will set my face like flint to do His will, and I know that I will triumph.

—Isaiah 50:7 (TLB)

One Monday morning, a friend gave me two badges to the Masters for the final round that concluded on Monday due to rain delays. After our nine o'clock class, Joel and I drove to our friend's apartment and literally dragged him out of bed to go to Augusta for the final round.

We arrived in Augusta and hurried breathlessly to the course just in time to see Jack Nicklaus begin his final day charge. Jack was eight shots back and needed a final round 64 to get in the hunt after a 77 the previous day. He birdied the first and second holes, and a huge crowd, hoping for some final round magic, followed Jack.

He parred the third and then inexplicably three-putted the par-3 fourth for a momentum-killing bogey. That would make the task really difficult now. I made my way to the ropes directly behind the fifth tee box as Jack and his caddie, Angelo Argea, walked over. Nicklaus, with his blond mane and unbelievable talent and strong work ethic, was on his way to becoming the greatest player in the history of the game.

Jack rarely showed strong emotion, but he was clearly perturbed by the three-putt. He rested his left arm on Angelo's shoulder and cleaned the grass out of his cleats using his divot repair tool.

Actually, he did more than clean the grass out. He ripped the grass out because he was still smoldering from the lost momentum. The fifth hole is a long, uphill par 4. Jack took a very aggressive line over the bunkers, set his jaw firmly with determination, and just smoked a BB over the bunker, setting up a short iron to the green, followed by two more birdies for a 32. He birdied the eighteenth hole to close with a 66, which would leave him two shots back.

Recalling how Jack set his jaw and dug down for something extra after the disappointing three-putt made me think about this verse from Isaiah. Sometimes, the Lord will give us a task to do, and we encounter dissension or lack of support or roadblocks that seemingly materialize out of nowhere. As believers, let's recall that we can set our jaw firmly and tap his great power through the Holy Spirit who lives within us. With God's power within us, we can overcome those obstacles and be victorious for his kingdom.

Prayer: Father, you never promised us that this life would be easy. When tough times come, remind me that your power is within me to face the difficulties and overcome them. Thank you, Lord. In Jesus's name, amen.

GOLF 06

Turning Tragedy into Triumph

Matthew 28:1–9, John 3:16–17

He is not here, He has risen, as He has said.

—Matthew 28:6

Ben Hogan was one of the greatest golfers in history. Known as the Ice Man for his steely concentration and quiet demeanor, Hogan overcame a great personal setback to play the best golf of his career three years after a near-fatal accident. In 1950, Hogan and his wife, Valerie, were hit head on by a bus on a dark, foggy road in Texas. Ben almost died, and his doctors considered tying off his legs, which would have left them useless. Though he made a miraculous recovery and was able to walk again, the doctors still said that he would never play competitive golf. But through tremendous perseverance and hard work, Hogan not only recovered but won the only three major championships that he entered in 1953. Tragedy was overcome by triumph to the delight of the sports world and his legion of fans.

Jesus showed all of us how tragedy was overcome by triumph. When he took a savage beating and was nailed to the cross, all hope appeared lost for his disciples and followers, who scattered after learning of his demise. His enemies jeered Jesus and cried, "Save yourself! Come down if you are the Son of God!" But Jesus triumphed over tragedy three days later when he rose from the grave and met two of his apostles on the road to Emmaus. He defeated death forever.

You can also overcome tragedy and live a triumphant life. God created a plan for your life to know him and experience joy as a believer, a person who has committed his life to Jesus Christ. Perhaps you have lost hope or seemingly lost your way. You can find your way to Christ through repentance and ask him to come into your life. Repentance, which is turning from sin and turning toward God, is absolutely necessary. Because without repentance, no matter how hard you try, your life will end in tragedy because you will be separated from God forever. When you die a physical death, you will also die spiritually if you don't know Christ. Turn tragedy into triumph and live eternally through trust and faith in Jesus Christ, the Living Son of God, and the One who took my place on the cross.

Prayer: Most holy God, giver of all good things, including the grace that I cannot earn, help me turn tragedy into triumph for eternity through your Son, Jesus Christ, who came into the world not to condemn me but to save me. In Jesus's name, amen.

A Tribute to Cora, Jack's Biggest Fan

Psalm 119:105, Jeremiah 6:16

Thy Word is a lamp unto my feet,
and a light unto my path.

—Psalm 119:105 (KJV)

I remember the first time that I saw my dear friend Cora. I was at my first Masters in 1973 when I was seventeen when I found out what a thrill it was to watch Jack Nicklaus, the Golden Bear, play golf for eighteen holes at Augusta. I decided to follow Jack on Saturday, but I didn't know the best way to get around the course. As Jack approached the green on the third hole to enthusiastic applause, I heard a high-pitched woman's voice. "Go get 'em, Jack!" Jack waved his hand in acknowledgment, and that's when I saw Cora. She was about five feet tall and was wearing a gold Jack's Pack pendant in the shape of a bear. Her beautiful silver hair was in a bun, and she wore sunglasses and a visor. She also seemed to know everybody around her.

As I walked the course, I found out it was tough to get close to Jack. On some holes, I would fall behind no matter how fast I walked to keep up. I would miss the timing for the crosswalk and be forced to wait for the group behind Jack to come through. Then I would hurry (without running, of course) to the next hole.

I kept noticing how this charming little woman was always in the right place. She didn't seem to be out of breath and chatted away until the next shot. So I got smart. *I will follow her, and then I'll be in the right place.* On the back nine, I introduced myself to Cora because I was a huge Jack fan, and she sort of adopted me from that point forward.

Cora walked almost every round with Jack for almost forty years beginning in 1963. She would pick his group up on number one fairway and follow him through his final putt on eighteen. Cora would record his putts for each hole on her program, and she never sat in the bleachers. After Jack completed his round, she walked home to nearby Cherry Lane. In 1986, I remember standing with her on seventeen when Seve Ballesteros hit his second shot in the water on fifteen, opening the door for Jack to win with a back nine thirty for his sixth green jacket. On seventeen came the putt when Jack lifts his putter in the air and Verne Lundquist screams, "Yes, sir!" I never saw anybody else at the Masters support Jack as loyally as Cora. She was indeed Jack's biggest fan at Augusta.

That sun-kissed Saturday afternoon at Augusta National began a wonderful friendship of about thirty-five years. After Cora could no longer walk the course, our family would still park in her yard on Cherry Lane and visit with her husband, affectionately known as "her Jack," and their daughter, Christy. When Cora passed away, Jack and Christy received a wonderful note from Barbara and Jack Nicklaus.

Cora had a specific path that she followed round after round (see Jeremiah 6:16) that put her in the best place to see the action. I wasted a lot of steps and energy trying to see the same action because of my lack of knowledge and experience. Psalm 119:105 says that the Word is a Lamp unto our feet and a Light unto our path. When we don't follow the teachings of the Word, we cost ourselves a lot of steps and energy. But if we learn the scriptures and follow the guidance provided there by God, we will be in the right place much more often. We will waste less energy in addressing the consequences that inevitably occur when we make bad decisions. Let's study his Word so that we will know the path of righteousness. When we stay on the right path, God blesses us with untold riches.

Prayer: Father God, thank you for the wonderful people we meet and the eternal relationships that we develop through sports. May I realize that sports is a wonderful gift that can be used to help people experience your mighty love. In the holy name of Jesus Christ, amen.

Note: Cora never wanted anyone to tie Jack's record of six Masters victories. When Tiger Woods came close to winning his fifth Masters one year, I found out why he lost when I got back to Cora's house: when Tiger would putt, Cora would put her thumb over the hole on TV so that the ball wouldn't go in.

GOLF 08

Does God Have a Tiger by the Tail?

1 Samuel 12:1–12, Psalm 41:4, 51:4

Against You, You only, have I sinned.

—Psalm 51:4

Tiger Woods was riding high at the top of his profession in the fall of 2009. Then came the stunning news that Tiger Woods was reported to be in serious condition in an Orlando hospital after an early morning car accident. This incorrect story was soon followed by a growing list of disturbing allegations of his unfaithfulness. Tiger's fall soon became a top news story around the world and the butt of countless jokes.

Tiger's idyllic life unraveled before his eyes. It would be really easy to give up on Tiger and throw him under the bus, but remember that God never gives up on us no matter how many times we mess up. When God looks at our personal sin, he doesn't weigh it or measure it. In God's eyes, sin is sin, period, and sin separates a person from God. He doesn't rank order it or compare it to the sins of other people as many are doing as they push Tiger below their names in the pecking order of worst sinners.

Despite his fame and fortune, Tiger is no different than you and me. You, Tiger, and I are all one on one with God. Any sins are between the individual and God. A believer should be in prayer for any person that has fallen. Before a person throws the next stone at someone, perhaps it's a good time to take stock to see if there is a speck in our left eye or a log in our right eye. Jesus taught us that lust is the same as adultery and hatred is the same as murder.

King David was also riding high. He was a man after God's own heart and was highly favored by God. David had conquered many tribes in recent battles. Perhaps he was complacent and bored on the day that he saw the stunning Bathsheba bathing on a rooftop. He had to have her, so he sent her husband, Uriah, into a dangerous battle and more or less instructed his army, "Okay. When the battle begins, on the count of three, everybody but Uriah take two big steps backward. Got it?" Uriah was killed, which paved the way for David to bring Bathsheba into the palace.

That's when God sent a man named Nathan to give David a little coaching. Nathan told David the story of a rich man who killed a poor man's only lamb, which crushed the poor man. David was appalled and called for the rich man to be put to death, but first, the rich man should repay the poor man with four ewes, David said. Nathan looked David in the eye and said, "You are the man."

Imagine the shivers that went through David's body and the sinking feeling in his stomach the instant that he realized how he had sinned against God. He cried out, "Against you alone, Lord, have I sinned." Nathan assured him that God would honor his confession and forgive his sins. David had lied to Uriah, coveted and stolen another man's wife, dishonored his family with his actions, and put his selfish desires above God and all that he knew to be honorable and virtuous. If the Ten Commandments represent ten bowling pins, David had just rolled a strike.

Will God grind Tiger to powder until he looks upward, thanks God for his mercy, and accepts God's free gift of grace available to all? I invite you to join me in praying that Tiger will repent and receive Christ. Consider the possibilities for God's kingdom. Many would be drawn to the Savior through evidence of fruit borne if Tiger's heart were changed by Christ. But first, Tiger must look heavenward and cry as David did, "Against You, You only, have I sinned."

Prayer: Dear Father God, help me learn from my mistakes and the mistakes of others so that I don't repeat them. I pray for salvation for Tiger and for those who don't know you as Savior. Help me let you do the judging, and I will do the praying. In Jesus's name, amen.

GOLF 09

Bernhard Langer

For the wages of sin is death, but the gift of God is
eternal life in Christ Jesus our Lord.

—Romans 6:23

Bernhard Langer began his golf career in Germany as a teenage apprentice and soon inherited the putting yips, which is an involuntary reflex that can send the ball speeding by the hole and off the green! He overcame that dilemma and later won golf's most prestigious event, the Masters Tournament, in 1985 and 1995. The soft-spoken German, who now resides in the United States, has achieved an illustrious career on the Champions Tour for golfers fifty and over. He shared this story of how he came to know Christ as his Savior.

> The week after I won the 1985 Masters, I was invited by a friend and fellow touring pro to come to the PGA Tour Bible Study.
>
> Something was missing. My priorities were golf, golf, more golf, then myself, and finally a little time with my wife. Every now and then, I prayed. I went to church. But if my golf game was not good,

my whole life was miserable and I made everyone around me miserable.

That night was the first time in my life that I heard that I needed to be "reborn." I was amazed to realize that the only way to have eternal life is through Jesus Christ—which he died for our sins. After understanding that God loved me so much that he sent his only Son to die for my sins, it was natural for me to ask the Lord into my life…I've seen tremendous changes in my life, my marriage, and my whole outlook. My priorities have changed. They're now where they should be: God first, family second, and then my career.

Prayer: Dear Jesus, thank you for this story of how we must be reborn to enter the kingdom of God. In fact, it's the same message that you shared with Nicodemus almost two thousand years ago. May I share with others that only through spiritual rebirth is it possible to enter the gates of heaven. In Jesus's name, amen.

GOLF 10

Larry Mize

I am the Vine, you are the branches. He who
abides in Me, and I in him, bears much fruit; apart
from Me you can do nothing.

—John 15:5

Larry Mize has enjoyed a successful career as a PGA Tour
professional and as a member of the Champions Tour. A
native of Augusta, Georgia, Larry dreamed as a young man
of being good enough to play in the Masters. Not only did
he achieve his first goal, but incredibly he won the major
championship, which he cherished more than any other.
On the second playoff hole of the 1987 Masters, Larry's
one-hundred-foot chip on the par-4 eleventh hole landed
on the green, checked, and rolled into the hole. He leaped
to celebrate one of golf history's biggest shots.

After that incredible win, a setback in his career occurred,
which he did not see coming. Two years later, Larry wanted
to quit golf because he was playing so poorly. He was think-
ing of himself as Larry Mize, Masters Champion, rather
than as a person who is capable of making mistakes. Then

Larry Moody, a Bible study leader on the PGA Tour, counseled him.

"Your significance doesn't come from being a professional golfer or a Masters champion…from what you've accomplished or what you do. It comes from knowing you're a child of God… That makes you significant no matter what the world says."

If only your job or performance makes you significant, then your life will be like a roller coaster because you will experience a series of ups and downs. You have infinite worth because God sent his only Son, Jesus Christ, to die for us.

Prayer: Father God, it seems that I'm grinding either because things aren't going well, or when they do, it is easy for me to get a swelled head. Help me stay grounded in the fact that becoming a Christian will always be the greatest thing that I have going for me. In Jesus's holy name, amen.

GOLF 11

Zach Johnson

By His stripes we are healed.

—Isaiah 53:5

Zach Johnson is a native of Iowa, who has enjoyed a great deal of success on the PGA Tour. He has won seven PGA Tour titles and was a Ryder Cup team member in 2006 and 2010.

Zach's two-shot victory over Tiger Woods at the 2007 Masters Tournament on Easter Sunday surprised those inside and outside the golf world but came as no surprise to those who know him. Johnson used the occasion to boldly proclaim his love and faith in Jesus Christ. He became the second professing Christian to win the Masters Tournament on Easter Sunday.

Johnson credited his faith in God and the counsel of longtime PGA Tour chaplain Larry Moody of Search Ministry, whose Bible study Johnson attends on a weekly basis, for allowing him to remain calm, cool, and collected in the competitive and often chaotic final round.

"Because it's Easter today, I want to say, 'Thank you, Jesus,'" Johnson said at the ceremony on the practice green.

"Being Easter Sunday, I feel very blessed and honored, and I feel like there was a power that was walking with me and guiding me. So that's where things stand. You know, I feel very blessed and honored to be here."

Zach beating Tiger down the stretch was sort of like David beating Goliath. When Zach faced his biggest moments on the back nine, he remembered that God was with him to give him strength and courage. When David slew Goliath, he was also conscious that God was by his side. Both of them gave God the glory.

Prayer: Father God, thank you for an athlete who thought about you during the most important tournament of his life. When I am under stress and there is a lot on the line, may I remember to include you and your power to keep me calm under pressure so that I can perform to the best of my ability. In Jesus's name, amen.

GOLF 12

Payne Stewart (1965–1999)

I have fought the good fight. I have finished the
race. I have kept the faith.

—2 Timothy 4:7

Payne Stewart was one of the most colorful golfers of his era. He was known for his stylish knickers that he wore to set himself apart from the other golfers. Payne was also quite a practical joker. When Paul Azinger, Payne's close friend, holed a bunker shot on the seventy-second hole to beat him by one at the 1993 Memorial Tournament, Payne was among the first people to congratulate him. After the press conference, Paul went back to the locker room to change into his street shoes, which were now full of mashed bananas, thanks to Payne!

Payne had come to a personal relationship with Jesus Christ not long before his life on earth came to a stunning end. It was a tragedy that sent shockwaves around the world. On October 25, 1999, a small plane plummeted to the ground near Mina, South Dakota, killing everyone aboard. Among them was golfing great Payne Stewart.

Just a few months earlier, he had captured the US Open in storybook fashion after a devastating loss in the same tournament the year before. Payne was best known among his peers for his flamboyant knickers, rhythmic golf swing, and the pranks that he pulled as a practical joker. But Payne had made huge strides in his faith earlier that year. When he accepted the trophy, he surprised many people by saying, "First of all, I have to give thanks to the Lord. If it weren't for the faith that I have in him, I wouldn't have been able to have the faith that I had in myself on the golf course...I'm proud of the fact that my faith in God is so much stronger, and I'm so much more at peace with myself than I've ever been in my life."

Often we are led to believe that improved performance on the athletic field comes strictly from working harder and practicing more. But Payne Stewart showed us that the key to winning the open was his growth in Christ that helped him keep his wits about him in golf's most pressure-packed event.

When Payne won the US Open on Father's Day, he obviously had no idea that he would leave this life behind less than six months later. The good news is that his wife and two children found some comfort because they knew Payne's final destination was the fairways of heaven. At Payne's memorial service, in recognition of his distinctive knickers, Paul Azinger paused at the podium and stuffed his pants legs into his socks in a tribute to his brother in Christ.

Prayer: Father God, thank you for the legacy of Payne Stewart, a man remembered not only for the joy with which he played the game of golf but for the joy that he received from finishing his race with Christ as his Lord. In Jesus's name, amen.

GOLF 13

Larry Nelson

But God demonstrates His own love toward us, in that while we were still sinners, Christ died for us.

—Romans 5:8

Larry Nelson is a three-time major championship winner and a member of the World Golf Hall of Fame. His legacy in golf is the quiet grace and humility that he has displayed while winning golf's most prestigious titles. Larry was named the winner of the 2011 PGA Distinguished Service award for his work with local charities.

Larry's career began unlike few others. After returning from a tour in Vietnam, he played golf for the first time at the age of twenty-one. He broke seventy in less than a year and earned his PGA Tour card in 1974. Larry shared the story of how he came to know Jesus Christ one year later.

The quiet Georgian was recuperating from an automobile accident in San Diego in 1975 and, with a hotel Bible in his hand, began to read. He recalled, "I had heard Billy Graham speak in Charlotte the year before and remembered that he said, 'If you have any questions about your relationship with the Lord, read the gospel of John and the book of Romans.'"

Nelson began to read in Romans and discovered that "all have sinned and come short of the glory of God." He realized that even though he had gone to church since he was a small child, he was not good enough to inherit eternal life on his own merits. After reading in Romans that Christ died for us while we were still sinners, Nelson asked Jesus to come into his life and experienced God's saving grace.

Larry's successful golf career shows us that it's never too late to find one's true talents in life. He used his skills effectively to put himself in a position to win two of golf's greatest championships. When he found himself with plenty of time on his hands in San Diego, he put himself in a position to receive eternal grace, God's greatest gift.

⛳

Prayer: Father God, thank you for the legacy of Larry Nelson and that not only will golf fans remember the majors that he won, but they will especially remember the demeanor of this champion who reflected the qualities of Christ regardless of whether he won or lost. In the holy name of Jesus Christ, amen.

GOLF 14

Paul Azinger

Jesus said to her, "I am the resurrection and the life.
Whoever believes in Me, though he die, yet shall
he live. And everyone who lives and believes in Me
shall never die. Do you believe this?"

—John 11:25–26

In 1993, Paul Azinger won the PGA Championship. He was at the height of his career, one of the top money winners on the tour. Then it happened. At age thirty-three, he was diagnosed with cancer, non-Hodgkin's lymphoma.

"A genuine feeling of fear came over me," he says. "I realized I could die. Everything I had accomplished in golf became meaningless to me. Then I remembered something that Larry Moody, who teaches a Bible study on the PGA Tour, said to me.

"Larry said, 'Zinger, we're not in the land of the living heading toward the land of the dying. We're in the land of the dying heading toward the land of the living.'"

Even the fear of death will step aside for someone who has the resurrection life of Jesus living inside them.

After Paul's successful battle with cancer, he came back to compete on the PGA Tour, became an ABC golf analyst, and later became the captain of America's winning Ryder Cup team in 2008.

Paul learned to place his trust in God, who has the power to heal us from cancer and other diseases. We will never know this side of heaven why some people are healed and some are not. But God understands when we are afraid; he hears our prayers and answers them according to his divine will.

Prayer: Most gracious Healer, help me to remember that you are the Great Physician and Healer. Thank you for brothers in Christ such as Larry Moody, who give me godly advice when I need it most. When I encounter a problem, may I remember to come to you for comfort and strength. In Jesus's name, amen.

GOLF 15

Stewart Cink

For God so loved the world, that He gave his only
begotten Son, that whosoever should believe in
Him, will not perish but have everlasting life.

—John 3:16 (KJV)

One of Stewart Cink's biggest claims to fame is that he was
the number one spoiler of Tiger Woods's unprecedented
amateur career. Stewart often beat Tiger or finished higher
than Tiger in important collegiate tournaments. A gradu-
ate of Georgia Tech, Stewart has won thirteen professional
tournaments worldwide, including the 2009 British Open
Championship. He has been a member of four President's
Cup teams and five Ryder Cup teams, including the victo-
rious 2008 Ryder Cup team.

In 2004, Stewart Cink and his pastor from Duluth First
Baptist Church traveled to Japan to do some mission work.
Many Japanese have an intense interest in golf and are
well-acquainted with top PGA celebrities. Consequently,
the six-foot-four-inch tall Cink used not only his physi-
cal height but his stature as a golfer as the platform upon

which to share his faith. Cink spoke to prominent business executives about golf and shared his testimony.

"Though it took me a few years, the most important lesson I ever learned was that the way to heaven leads directly through Jesus Christ and only through Him," Cink testifies. "My relationship with Christ is now the central part of my life. I am a better father to my two boys. I am a better husband to my wife, and I am a better golfer now that the Lord is walking with me in the fairways and through the rough."

Prayer: Father God, help me realize as Stewart did that the closer that I am in knowing Christ, the better person I will become in all of my personal relationships. Thank you for the most important relationship of all, which is the eternal one with Jesus. In Jesus's name, amen.

GOLF 16

Tom Lehman

When someone becomes a Christian, he becomes a
new person inside. He is not the same anymore. A
new life has begun!

—2 Corinthians 5:17 (TLB)

After playing college golf at the University of Minnesota,
Tom Lehman survived the rigors of playing second-tier
golf tours in the United States and even the Asian Tour
before finally earning his card on the PGA Tour.

His biggest tournament win came at the prestigious
1996 British Open Championship with his father in
attendance. But his win led to an assurance that no worldly
victory, no matter how exciting, can ever approach the ulti-
mate victory of knowing Jesus Christ. Here is how Tom
recalls the experience.

> I'll never forget the day I won the British Open, all
> the awards ceremonies, the champagne toast with
> the R & A, the endless interviews. What a feeling
> of exhilaration!
>
> Winning the British Open was a thrill of a life-
> time. But I learned a long time ago that the thrill

of victory is fleeting. It's not long before you find yourself asking, "What's next?"

As much as I longed to win a major championship, it didn't change anything. I was still the same person as before. I had the same hang-ups, the same problems, and even some new ones.

The Bible says, "All men are like grass and their glory is like the flowers of the field. The grass withers and the flowers fall."

So what is it that lasts? The only thing that has given my life true meaning: my relationship with Jesus Christ.

Lehman learned that even winning one of the ultimate championships in golf pales in comparison to knowing Christ as your Savior and Lord and to have the peace and assurance that God is with you each day of your life.

Prayer: Dear Father, thank you for the lesson to be learned of staying grounded in Christ no matter how thrilling our victories are in this world. I thank you for the ultimate victory of knowing Christ and being in heaven with him one day. In the holy name of Jesus, amen.

GOLF 17

Kenny Perry

Be glad for all that God is planning for you. Be
patient in trouble and prayerful always.

—Romans 12:12

When Kenny Perry attempted to qualify for the PGA
Tour, he agreed to a unique sponsorship. A man gave him
five thousand dollars for qualifying school. If he failed to
qualify, he didn't have to pay it back. If he qualified, he
agreed to give 5 percent of his earnings to David Lipscomb
University in Nashville, Tennessee. Kenny has honored this
pledge throughout his career.

It looked like a storybook ending to cap a career that
blossomed late. Kenny Perry experienced the thrill of a life-
time in his home state of Kentucky, when he played well as
a member of the first victorious US Ryder Cup Team in a
decade. He had four wins on the PGA Tour in the eighteen
months leading up to the 2009 Masters. Kenny was one par
away from being the oldest man to win the Masters after
stuffing an 8-iron within six inches of the cup on the leg-
endary sixteenth hole. But Kenny was unable to finish off

his round, and he bogeyed the last two holes and eventually lost in a playoff.

However, Kenny allowed the Lord's light to shine during the playoff when he applauded Angel Cabrera's miracle par save from the trees and again when he was incredibly gracious after perhaps the most disappointing hour of his golf career. Kenny said after his heartbreaking loss, "I have got my mom struggling with cancer, my dad's struggling [with his heart]. I have got a lot of people who are hurting right now and here I am playing golf for a living and having the time of my life. So I'm not going there. I'm not going to play 'pity on me.' And you know what? I'm going to enjoy it. I really am. I fought hard and I was proud of the way I hung in there."

Kenny demonstrated that God's grace can surface during a time of significant disappointment. He honored his parents and maintained his perspective that there is much more to life than winning a major golf tournament.

Prayer: Father God, in a day when so many athletes and coaches are less than gracious in defeat, thank you for the lessons of generosity, humility, and good sportsmanship from Kenny Perry. Help me keep my victories and defeats in proper perspective to my loved ones around me. In Jesus's name, amen.

GOLF 18

Gary Player

Give thanks for everything to our God and Father
in the name of our Lord Jesus Christ.

—Ephesians 5:20

Gary Player is a nine-time major championship winner who has flown millions of miles around the world in his fifty-plus years in professional golf. He has traveled more miles than any golfer and played in more Masters tournaments (fifty-one) than any player in history. Gary played his final round in the Masters on the Friday of the 2009 tournament. The fans applauded him at each green for being a three-time Masters champion and for the determination and humility that he consistently displayed.

This question came from a writer after his last Masters round: "Can you remember the reception you had on the eighteenth? Was that louder than when you won all your jackets?"

Gary replied, "No question. Ten times more. I'll never forget that as long as I live. It just went on and on and on from all sides."

He continued, "But it happened on every single hole. All thirty-six holes, I got a standing ovation. I wish I had words to…I wish, as I had just mentioned, the vocabulary of Winston Churchill to say the correct thing, but it was a feast. It was something you'll never, ever forget. You'll go to your grave knowing you had tremendous love showered upon yourself."

Gary said, "I'm saying it, and I'm repeating myself, that I said it at the dinner the other night. We can all say a prayer, and everybody has a choice of believing or not, but a man never stands so tall as when he's on his knees."

Player received tributes around the course that day. In front of the final green, he got on his knees and gave God the glory, the honor, and the praise.

Prayer: Father God, thank you for the legacy of Gary Player, a man small in stature but a giant among his peers for his accomplishments both on and off the golf course. May I be reminded that when I want to stand tall, I need to make it happen on my knees. In the precious name of Jesus, amen.

GOLF 19

Pat Summerall (1930–2013)

You will seek Me and find Me when you seek Me
with all your heart.

—Jeremiah 29:13 (NIV)

Pat Summerall was a professional football player for the New York Giants in the 1950s, but he is better known for his career as a broadcaster. Ironically he began his broadcasting career after fielding a phone call for his teammate, Giants quarterback Charley Connerly. A TV station called to invite Connerly to try out for a broadcasting job, and Pat talked the station into giving him an audition too!

Pat eventually became one of the all-time great sportscasters, and he called thirty Masters tournaments for CBS Sports. He was well-known for being able to paint the big picture by saying more with fewer words. Everything seemed to come easy for Pat since his rise as a sportscaster.

But Pat glorified in himself and eventually became an alcoholic. He was shocked into entering the Betty Ford clinic when his daughter said she was ashamed to share his last name. After stubbornly entering the clinic, Pat began to read the Bible and kept reading it after leaving the clinic thirty-three days later. (The first five days didn't count; he was so angry.)

He committed his life to Christ in 1992 and underwent a liver transplant in 2004. After expressing guilt over someone else dying so that he could live, his pastor replied, "Because God is not done with you yet!"

In his first visit to Augusta since his liver transplant, Pat triumphantly but humbly returned for Masters week 2009 and gave his testimony to over a thousand people at the prayer breakfast on Masters Tuesday.

Pat and all of us can be thankful that we serve a God who never gives up on us and will never stop pursuing us, no matter how far we have strayed from him.

Prayer: Father God, thank you for your pursuit of me that never ends. You never give up on me regardless of how badly I have messed up. Thank you for your eternal promise of a life in Christ if only I will hold up my end of the deal. In Jesus's name, amen.

GOLF 20

Up and Down

His mercies are new every morning.

—Lamentations 3:23

One key to making a good score in golf is to be a good chipper and putter. Even the best players miss the green with their approach shots a third of the time, or six out of eighteen holes. There is nothing like a great pitch and a well-holed eight-footer to give you momentum and keep your round going. Getting it up on the green and down in one putt is called an up and down.

When I played on my college golf team, my roommate, Tim Fulcher, was our number 1 player, not because he hit the ball further than anyone but because he could chip and putt with the best of them. During my sophomore season, we played in a regional championship at Stone Mountain, and one of his competitors was muttering to himself as he approached the eighteenth green. When someone asked him what the matter was, he whined, "That guy [Tim] could get it up and down out of a trash can!" Fulcher had gotten it up and down seven times on the back nine on his way to winning individual medalist honors.

Another player who was pretty doggone good at getting it up and down was Tom Watson. Jack Nicklaus was gunning for a record fifth US Open Championship, and he and Watson were tied. Watson hooked his approach shot to the left of the green into tall rough, but he drew a favorable lie. When his caddie, Bruce Edwards, encouraged him to chip it close, Watson said, "Close? I'm gonna make it." He did and ran a victory lap around the green, pointing at Bruce Edwards in an "I told you so!" gesture of happiness and exultation.

Just as an up and down is important for golfers to maintain good scores, an up and down is important for believers to maintain good standing with God. Too often, when we are up, when things are going exceedingly well, we forget to get down on our knees and thank God for the abundant blessings that he gives us each day. We need to remember that each day he gives us is a blessing in itself and that our mercies are new every morning. When we are down because of circumstances, we can be lifted up by the joy that comes from knowing that Christ understands and has been through whatever we're going through. Jesus also intercedes on our behalf, and the Holy Spirit supplies a deeper understanding of what we are really trying to tell God when the right words just won't come out.

So remember, the simple key to an up and down for a believer is being on our knees when we are up and being on our knees when we are down. That's how you build a lasting relationship with the Father.

Prayer: Dear Father, when I need to be lifted up, help me get down on my knees. Only your love, mercy, and grace can lift me up. I thank you for your saving grace from which I can draw joy each day. In the holy name of the Risen One, amen.

GOLF 21

What Really Matters

When someone becomes a Christian, he becomes
a new person inside. He is not the same anymore, a
new life has begun!

—2 Corinthians 5:17 (TLB)

I was watching the AT&T Pebble Beach National Pro-Am on TV, and a tribute to the late Danny Gans appeared on the screen. Sadly, Danny Gans had passed away last Pro-Am, and the final credit read "Danny Gans (1956–2009)." I reflected that Danny and I probably shared several similarities: First of all, a love for golf and a love for Pebble Beach, one of the world's most breathtaking golf courses. He and I shared the same first name: Danny. We were both fathers. We both had four letters in our last names. He and I were virtually the same age when he passed. I was born in 1955, and he was born in 1956. One similarity that we did not share is that he apparently made millions of dollars per year as an impersonator in the Las Vegas casinos.

One of the most glorious meetings of land and sea is how Pebble Beach has long been described. I had the good fortune of attending the AT&T Pebble Beach Pro-Am tournament in 2000 and 2001 and playing several area courses. What a thrill it was to be part of the spectacle as a spectator. It was a sun-kissed Saturday, the surf was crashing along the par five eighteenth, it was seventy-two degrees when there was snow in the east, and the stars of golf and entertainment were on display. The entertainers joked with the crowds, signed autographs, and occasionally hit a decent shot or made a putt. The tournament ended at 3:00 p.m. in the west since TV needed a 6:00 p.m. finish in the east.

One of the coolest golf moments that I ever had was sitting on the seventh tee after tournament play had concluded. I was facing Carmel Bay and listening to stories about the tournament from one of the groundskeepers. For a golf fan, it doesn't get much better.

I was almost three years from being saved the last time I went to the AT&T Pebble Beach Pro-Am. At the time, I lived for moments like Pebble Beach to fill the God-shaped vacuum in my heart. When I experienced a great sports thrill, I wanted another one. But after I was saved, moments like that didn't hold the same attraction. I am grateful that I experienced Pebble and Augusta National, but if I never went back, it would be okay. Events like that just don't grab me like they once did. It has everything to do with my attitude in Christ once I received him. It's his eternal moments that I attempt to live for.

I never knew Danny Gans, but I hoped that at that moment, there was life in eternity for him with God, beyond the ice plants and crashing waves of Pebble Beach, a very special place.

Prayer: Father God, it's cool when I get to do neat stuff and call my friends and brag to them about where I am. But help me keep the right perspective and include you there with me to enjoy the moment. I praise you for the special opportunities that I have through sports and hope that I honor you during those good times. In Jesus's name, amen.

GOLF 22

Heaven's Grand Slam (Golf)

*Jeremiah 29:11, Romans 5:8, 1 John 1:9,
John 3:16, Ephesians 2:8*

But by grace you have been saved through faith.

—Ephesians 2:8

Each year, the best golfers in the world attempt to achieve immortality in golf's history book by winning one of the four major championships. It's only happened once that a golfer won all four majors in the same year. That feat was achieved by the incomparable sportsman and gentleman, Bobby Jones from Atlanta, Georgia, in 1930. His dear friend, the writer O. B. Keeler, chronicled Bobby's greatest triumphs and named the achievement the impregnable quadrilateral. Now the feat is called the Grand Slam. In 1930, the Grand Slam consisted of the US Amateur, the US Open, the British Open, and the British Amateur tournaments. After achieving the Grand Slam, Bobby retired from competitive golf at the age of thirty and later founded the Masters Golf Tournament, which became one of the four majors along with the US Open, the British Open, and the PGA Championship.

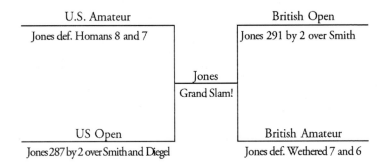

Bobby Jones 1930 Grand Slam of Golf

U.S. Amateur	British Open
Jones def. Homans 8 and 7	Jones 291 by 2 over Smith

Jones
Grand Slam!

US Open	British Amateur
Jones 287 by 2 over Smith and Diegel	Jones def. Wethered 7 and 6

Just as the golf Grand Slam consists of four major tournaments, there are four key principles that every person needs to understand about salvation. First, you are wonderfully and uniquely made (Psalm 139:14) by God, and God created a unique plan (Jeremiah 29:11) for your life so that you can enjoy his special blessings. The unique plan doesn't mean everything that happens to us will be wonderful and that we will live without problems.

Second, each person is separated from God from the first time that he or she consciously breaks one of the Ten Commandments. Each person inherits a sinful nature at birth (Psalm 51:5) and is destined to commit his or her first sin at an early age, which separates us from God. Everyone who has ever lived has experienced this sinful separation from God (Romans 3:23), and if we don't do something about it, spiritual death (Romans 6:23) will be the end.

Third, God loved us so much in spite of our shortcomings that even while we were sinners (Romans 5:8), he sent Jesus to be the bridge over the chasm of sin that separates us from God. Jesus even bore our sin in his body when he went to the cross (1 Peter 2:24). But the good news that we celebrate every day is that Jesus left the tomb and came back to life (Matthew 28:6).

The great news is that, unlike having to win each of the four legs of the golf Grand Slam, God already took care of the first three legs of heaven's Grand Slam. You only need to achieve the fourth and final leg to win heaven's Grand Slam. You must make the decision to exchange your sinful life for a new life in Christ. You must repent, or turn from your sinful life, and ask God to forgive you (1 John 1:9). After you repent, you must trust and accept God's gift of grace to receive eternal life (Ephesians 2:8). By placing your faith in Jesus Christ, you admit once and for all that you cannot earn God's grace and that salvation only comes through Jesus Christ (John 3:16). Then grow in Christ and obedience to God by praying frequently and studying his Word daily. This next sentence is important: put Christ first in all aspects of your life (Proverbs 3:6) so that he will become your Lord.

God offers everyone his free gift of grace. You can pray to receive Jesus Christ into your life as your Savior. Your attitude and change of heart is more important than these exact words.

Prayer: Lord Jesus, I need you. Thank you for suffering on the cross and dying for my sins. I want my life to change. Please forgive all my sins through Christ's blood that was spilled for me. Jesus, I ask you to come into my heart. Thank you for your free gift of grace and eternal life with you in heaven. Thank you for the Holy Spirit that helps me any time of the night or day. May I grow in obedience and Christlikeness through prayer and Bible study. Thank you for accepting me as a child in the family of God. In the precious name of Jesus I pray. Amen.

Now consider these statements carefully. You cannot receive Jesus without admitting your sins and vowing to turn away from your sinful life. If you understand each statement and really want to commit to each, you should pray and ask Christ into your heart in your own words. Write your name under *Saint*. You should receive the Holy Spirit and eternal life through Jesus Christ if you were sincere and understood your commitment.

Heaven's Grand Slam

Step 1) God's Plan for Man

Psalm 139:14; Jeremiah 29:11

(Wonderfully Made; Plan for Good)

Step 3) Jesus Died for My Sin

Romans 5:8; 1 Peter 2:24; Matthew 28:6

(Loved sinner; My Sin His Body; Jesus is Risen)

Saint

Step 2) My Sinful Self

Exodus 20:3; Romans 3:23;Romans 6:23

(Self idol; All sinned; Apart from God)

Step 4) Repent, Trust, Obey

1 John 1:9; Eph. 2:8; John 3:16; Prov. 3:5-6

(Cleansed; Grace: Eternal Life; All Your Ways)

Check box if you sincerely intend to:

☐ Repent (turn from) all of your sin.

☐ Trust Jesus Christ as your Savior and Lord. Obey God by praying and studying his Word.

☐ If you checked all three boxes, pray now for Jesus Christ to come into your heart. Write your name in the box under *saint*. Welcome to God's family as His child.

GOLF 23

A Reluctant but Wise Decision

Jonah 3, Romans 8:26

And the word of the Lord came to Jonah,
the second time, saying, "Arise, go to Ninevah,
that great city, and preach to it the preaching that
I bid you."

—Jonah 3:1–2

My coaching friend and golf buddy, AG, shared this gem with me.

AG coached high school basketball and golf for thirty years, but he had never been fortunate enough to hang a Georgia High School Association banner in his gym for either a state champion or runner-up team. His boys' golf team was locked in a tight battle for second place, and he wanted to hang a banner in what could possibly be his final competition "more than he could describe," he told me.

One of his players finished his afternoon round and told AG that he had shot 76. AG reminded him to check his scorecard and turn it in. Under the rules of golf, turning in the scorecard ended the player's responsibility. He headed to the scorer's table, and AG waited for his last two golfers to finish.

A few minutes later, another player came over and told AG that the player who shot 76 was on the board for a 74. AG went to the scorer's table and told the GHSA official that he thought there was a problem. The GHSA official pulled his card, and sure enough, it was a 76. AG told the GHSA official, "If my team loses because of those two shots, get all the razor blades away from me." Sure enough, his team finished third by two shots.

Looking back, AG would love to tell you that he never hesitated, but part of him was screaming, "Don't do it! It's in the rules!" the whole time. But he knew that the kids would *know* every time they came in that gym that the banner was for a mistake. He felt trapped with no good way out. During the entire five-hour ride home that night from Jekyll Island, Coach was really down, but he knew that he did the only thing God would permit him to do. There was nowhere to hide and nothing to hide behind, and he knew it.

AG believes that God gives kids to coaches so that they have the chance to be good role models in spite of their imperfections because of who he is and who he wants us to be, even though we're not the people that we will be until the day when we are made perfect in Christ.

He shared with me that his situation reminded him of Jonah's story. Just as AG might have initially been reluctant to go to the scorer's table and deny the 74, Jonah was very reluctant to go to Nineveh and even wound up barfed up on the beach after three days in a whale's belly. But Coach still came through with the right decision, and God still found a way to prompt Jonah to prophesy to the people of Nineveh and save 120,000 people from his wrath.

Prayer: Father God, thank you for the Holy Spirit that prompts us as believers to do the right thing, even when we are torn by our selfish desires to act in another way. In Jesus's holy name, amen.

GOLF 24

The Augusta Press Conference

Psalm 7:11–13, Romans 2:1–16, 2 Peter 2:9

The Lord knows how to deliver the godly out of
temptations, and to reserve the unjust to the day of
judgment to be punished.

—2 Peter 2:9

A most unusual event in the history of the Masters was
scheduled for the Monday of the 2010 Masters. Tiger
Woods held his first press conference that was truly open to
the press since his startling allegations of adultery became
public. The interview room was jam-packed with more
than two hundred golf writers on what is usually a very
casual day as golfers get in their first official practice round.

Tiger was introduced by the moderator from Augusta
National and answered exactly forty questions over thirty-
four minutes from the golf media who had waited anx-
iously to ask their specific questions. The details and cir-
cumstances surrounding Tiger's admitted transgressions
were once again chronicled three days before he tackled
Augusta National, which is a challenge under any circum-

stances. Millions renewed their opinions of Tiger amid the fallout that he created for himself.

You had better believe that this press conference was a tough situation. But one day, you could find yourself in a situation that is much tougher and infinitely more important and fearful. That is when you take the stand at the Day of Judgment. How would any of us answer God's forty most probing questions of our personal lives? Each man and woman passes from this earth and comes before God one on one at the throne of our most holy God.

Unless Jesus takes the microphone from our hands and says, "[Your Name], you can leave now. Well done, good and faithful servant. I will take it from here." That is the beauty of Judgment Day when you are a believer. Jesus will handle Judgment Day with God for you, and you will never have to face God. That alone is worth coming to Christ, isn't it? If you are not a believer, one who has earnestly repented and accepted Christ as your Savior, then you are in for one tough press conference. How could a person ever justify and explain to God about the times that he or she has been unfaithful and wasted time chasing the trappings and lures of the world? What a relief it is to know as followers of Christ that Jesus will speak on our behalf at the pearly gates. This type of press conference is inevitable. Prepare now.

Prayer: Father God, thank you for the perfect goodness of your mercy and grace that Jesus can represent me, a sinner washed in the blood of the Lamb. I pray to you now that [insert a friend's name] who will face you on Judgment day will come to know Jesus Christ as Savior and Lord. In Jesus's name, amen.

GOLF 25

Rope Trick

Draw near to God, and He will draw near to you.

—James 4:8

It is very difficult to get near the best players at Augusta National during the Masters due to the immense crowds, particularly in the last ten years as portions of the course have been cordoned off to give the players more privacy on certain holes such as eight, fifteen, and sixteen. But there are ways to get up close and personal to see your favorite players and follow the leaders on the back nine on Sunday. Here are several techniques that I've learned over the years.

1. Stay half a hole ahead. When the player tees off, you need to be up the fairway near the point where the ball will roll to a stop. Then you have a perfect view of the approach to the green.

2. The rope trick. When people are walking up the fairway ahead of you in the gallery, push against the rope with your thigh. The rope will give about two feet, which is just enough room to pass people on the left. You'll zoom past them like a NASCAR driver on the back straightaway.

3. Wanna get close to your favorite player and on TV? Go to the ball when it goes in the rough. A huge crowd of people will surround the ball, and the marshal will ask everyone to step back. What you do is put your foot out, stand sideways, and brace yourself. When people start to back up, they will bump into the wedge that you've created, and people will part on your left and right. You'll be on the front row with a perfect view of the action.

Sounds like a lot of trouble? It is. You've really got to work hard if you want to see the action. Aren't you glad that we don't have to work that hard to be in intimate contact with God? There is no need to get ahead of him; it works best when we are in step with his perfect timing. We don't have to wait in lines and fight the crowds. Somehow, he is able to handle everybody's needs simultaneously. Want to get close to God? He loves you immeasurably, and he's waiting to meet you right now in the Word or through prayer, which is just plain talking to him. Draw near to God, and he will draw near to you (James 4:8).

Prayer: Dearest Holy Father, help me realize that the words don't have to be perfect when I come to you. You just want to spend time with me, and the Holy Spirit will help me with the words. Thank you for being so understanding of my shortcomings. I love you, Father. In the name of Jesus, amen.

GOLF 26

Prediction

Who has believed our report? And to whom has
the arm of the Lord been revealed?

—Isaiah 53:1

One of my favorite golf experiences is to watch the major
championships on TV, especially on Sunday. The second
major of the year, the US Open, always falls on Father's
Day. My wife and daughters have been sweet enough over
the years to watch the US Open with me. One of my fond-
est memories is when the late Jim McKay of ABC would
open the telecast with a dramatic welcome to the ninety-
fifth playing of the United States Open, a national cham-
pionship conducted by the United States Golf Association.

When you've watched thousands of hours of golf on TV
as I have, you begin to learn some of the nuances of the
broadcasters. I really get into it and love to predict what
will happen next. I would even do some ad lib color com-
mentary of my own. I might see a player trailing by two
with four holes to play. He's on a par five playing down-
wind, and I would mutter, "He needs to make birdie." Two
seconds later, the announcer would say, "He needs to make
birdie." Allison and Jillian would look at me and say, "Why

aren't you doing this?" The wind at Royal Birkdale is whipping into the golfers at thirty miles per hour on a long par 4, and I would say, "He needs to drive it in the fairway to get home in two. " Ditto from the announcer. Perhaps the golfer's iron shot did not produce the distinctive click of a well-struck shot, and I would say, "That needs to get up." Then I get the look from the girls as my echo chimes in.

Just as the announcer occasionally echoed my words, Jesus often repeated the words of the prophets, and particularly Isaiah seemed to be his favorite. Jesus quoted the prophets so that the people of New Testament days could make the connection between his coming as the Messiah and the prophecies from the Old Testament that were shared by Isaiah, Micah, and the authors of the Psalms. The prophets foretold the people what would happen during their day and hundreds of years from now. The evidence of prophecies helps make a strong case for the birth, the miracles, the death, and the resurrection of Jesus Christ.

Prayer: Father God, thank you for the many prophets who foretold the coming of Christ and the details of his death and resurrection. Help me realize that it takes the stories of the prophets to complete the picture that you need us to understand. In the holy and beautiful name of Jesus Christ, our precious Savior and Lord, amen.

GOLF 27

The Rules of Golf

Exodus 20:1–19

You shall have no other gods before Me.

—Exodus 20:3

Adherence to the rules of golf is essential to the integrity of the game. The rules of golf are determined by the Royal and Ancient Golf Club of St. Andrews and the United States Golf Association. The rules uphold the integrity of the game, and it is up to players to play by those rules strictly or face the consequences of penalties.

Several situations involving violations of the rules of golf stand out. Once, Bobby Jones called a one-stroke penalty on himself when he and he alone saw his ball move after he grounded his club. His comment? "You might as well congratulate me for not robbing a bank." In the 1968 Masters, Roberto De Vicenzo lost the tournament when he signed for a lower score on the seventeenth hole because of a mistake made by his playing partner, Tommy Aaron, who inadvertently wrote down the wrong score. De Vicenzo signed for an incorrect score and was disqualified. His comment? "What a stupid I am!"

God gives us ten rules in the Bible to follow, and when we violate them, we suffer the consequences just like these golfers did. God sent the *Ten* Commandments through Moses from Mount Sinai to give the people of Israel rules for living and obeying him. Ten simple rules for living, and if you break any of them, you're separated from God.

One day, God sent Jesus to be the Savior, the long-awaited Messiah of the people of Israel, and eventually, he also became the Savior of the Gentiles (non-Jews). The reason? No matter how hard we try, we cannot keep the rules that he gave us to live by. So he sent a Savior to atone for our sins, and as believers, we should celebrate the Risen One each day.

Prayer: Thank you, Father, for the Ten Commandments, our rules to live by. May I know the spirit and intent of these rules and use them as my schoolmaster. In Jesus's name, amen.

On the Back Nine of Life

Hebrews 10:17, Romans 8:1

I will never again remember their sins and
lawless deeds.

—Hebrews 10:17 (TLB)

The following golf scorecard depicts the average life span. Par is seventy-two, and the average life span is about seventy-two years. Every four years of your life constitutes one hole, so thirty-six years are nine holes. If you're older than thirty-six, do you realize you are on the back nine of life? That should be a sobering thought. I'm fifty-five, so I'm halfway through the back nine. What if you could play number four again when you were age thirteen through sixteen or number eight again when you were age twenty-nine through thirty-two?

If you've gone to pgatour.com to check the tournament leaderboards, you'll recognize the color codes. Red is birdie, par is white, but the bluer you get, the bigger the mess you made. Here is a typical scorecard of a recreational golfer.

Hole	1	2	3	4	5	6	7	8	9	Out	10	11	12	13	14	15	16	17	18	In	Total
Par	4	5	4	3	5	3	4	4	4	36	4	5	3	4	5	4	4	3	4	36	72
Score	4	6	5	5	4	5	8	6	5	48	4	6	5	5	5	7					

How many of us have ruined a good golf game by losing our cool over one lousy shot? We're still thinking about it four or five holes later as we double bogey ourselves into oblivion. We miss a short putt, and we're looking back three holes later at the green where we missed the short putt. As if that will do any good.

Sometimes we do that with our lives, berating ourselves or wearing ourselves out with guilt and anger over past hurts from fifteen to twenty years ago. We don't ask God for forgiveness so that we can move on, or if we ask God for forgiveness, we don't accept his forgiveness. We ask him and take it back, ask him and take it back again and again, like a broken record.

When we finally realize that Jesus Christ is the only way to find joy and stability in our lives and we fully repent and God washes us as pure as snow, guess what the Father does to our scorecard? He wipes away all of our bogeys, double bogeys, and triple bogeys and gives us the Holy Spirit (God in us) for eternity and the free gift of eternal life. He doesn't just forgive; he forgets as if the sin had never happened.

When we get in lock step with him, we're making birdies and eagles and pars the rest of our days until we are made perfect in Jesus Christ. Oh, there will still be mistakes and bogeys and such, but he will turn a triple into a par and a par into an eagle. Because all our mistakes are forgiven when we turn to the cross, repent, and ask for forgiveness. We are forgiven seventy times seven, and God will forgive us infinitely when we ask him. We are no longer held in condemnation for our sins after we become believers.

Here is your scorecard in Christ after you become a believer.

Hole	1	2	3	4	5	6	7	8	9	Out	10	11	12	13	14	15	16	17	18	In	Total
Par	4	5	4	3	5	3	4	4	4	36	4	5	3	4	5	4	4	3	4	36	72
Score	4	5	4	3	4	3	4	4	4	35	4	5	3	4	5	4	1	2	3	31	66

It's your choice for the next shot for your next hole in life as you decide which club to pull out of your bag. I'm on the fourteenth hole. I've got a hard left-to-right wind, it's uphill, it's late in the day, the sun is in my eyes, and my hands are cold. I've got the bad memories of past failures, such as blocking the shot into the hazard on the right. But I choose to place my trust in Jesus. I hit my tee ball long and straight, stuffed a wedge to three feet, and will sink that birdie putt. I go to the fifteenth hole with a brave new attitude and keep trusting in him. You have a choice too, and I pray to our Almighty God that you decide to pull the right club before your round ends.

Prayer: Father God, help me salvage my life round today no matter what hole I'm on. I repent and take full advantage of your forgiveness. May I truly believe that no matter what sin I have committed, you will forgive and forget. I need to let go of past failures and let you forgive me. In Jesus's name, amen.

GOLF 29

Dustin's Warning Signs

2 Timothy 3:16, Psalm 119:100–109

All scripture is given by inspiration of God, and is
profitable for doctrine, for reproof, for correction,
for instruction in righteousness.

—2 Timothy 3:16

Make no mistake. The game of golf is alive and well. For those who were concerned that there were no exciting players beyond the post-Tiger/Phil era, the 2010 PGA Championship was truly a changing of the guard. The back nine play at Whistling Straits generated riveting drama. Six players, including three who were twenty-five or younger, had a great chance to win over the last three holes, producing one of the most thrilling shootouts since Jack Nicklaus won his final major championship in the 1986 Masters.

Nick Watney, a twenty-something rising star, entered the last round with a three-shot lead, but his game fell apart on Sunday's front nine. Steve Elkington, a member of the old guard at forty-seven, missed two easy putts that would have given him the lead. Bubba Watson, the crowd-pleasing bomber wearing his emotions on his sleeve, blasted 390-

yard drives and displayed the deft touch of a safe cracker. Golf's next superstar, twenty-one-year-old Rory McIlroy, finished one shot back along with Zach Johnson, winner of the 2007 Masters. Eventually, twenty-five year-old Martin Kaymer of Germany beat Bubba in a three-hole playoff.

The playoff was somewhat anticlimactic because the lead story of the 2010 PGA Championship was twenty-five-year-old Dustin Johnson, another prodigious long-ball hitter. Dustin came to the eighteenth hole with a one-shot lead after tremendous birdies on sixteen and seventeen. He drove outside the ropes into a bunker that had been trampled all week by spectators. Dustin grounded his club in the bunker and was assessed a two-shot penalty by the PGA rules officials, thereby missing the playoff by one stroke.

Much to his credit, Dustin reacted like a gentleman when he received the ruling. He didn't go ballistic or blame the PGA officials, saying that they had their job to do.

Whistling Straits is a unique golf course because there are hundreds of sand bunkers outside the ropes on this links-style layout. Prior to the beginning of play, the PGA ruled that all sandy areas would be played as bunkers. That ruling meant that a player cannot touch the sand in the bunker with his club before striking it. The two-shot penalty, viewed as too harsh by many people, should not have been a surprise to Dustin or any golfer in the field because the PGA officials posted a sheet of tournament rules in large font on the players' locker room mirrors.

Watney commented afterward that the players generally don't read the rules much. Usually, when a player is concerned about committing a rules infraction on tour, he simply summons a rules official. Think about someone posting a message on the front door so that you couldn't possibly miss it in the morning. The reminder on the locker room mirrors read in part: "Bunkers: All areas designed and built as sand bunkers will be played as bunkers (hazards). Many bunkers will likely include numerous footprints, heel prints, and tire tracks. No free relief will be available."

Initially, I felt tremendous sympathy toward Dustin regarding the ruling, especially considering the chaos in the gallery surrounding him on eighteen. Nevertheless, he failed to ask for a rules official, consult his rulebook, or confer with his caddie before grounding his club. Dustin obviously failed to heed the special warnings that the PGA posted in the locker room. Admittedly, he had not taken time to read and understand the warning. The oversight cost him a shot at winning the ensuing playoff of golf's final major of the year. Dustin clearly suffered the consequences for his mistake.

Many people don't read God's rules much either. Certainly God blessed us with a conscience to know right from wrong, and believers have the additional advantage of the prompting of the Holy Spirit when we are about to mess up. When we hit the ball into trouble, we can consult the Rule Book (God's Word) or call in the Rules Official (Holy

Spirit) to help us make the proper decision. Back in the day, God gave the people of Israel special warnings through the pleas of a dozen major and minor prophets. These men told the chosen ones to repent or face the consequences of eternal separation from God. Jesus spoke often in the Gospels of the eternal consequences of failing to heed the warnings of the prophets. God still places people and circumstances in our paths. These events are warnings that tell us we need to turn to God, whether we recognize them or not.

Have you heeded the special warnings? Take time now to respond to the warning signs. Your response could make the difference in winning or losing your final major.

Prayer: Father God, when you woo me to change, thank you for giving me many warning signs. Help me heed these signs so that I am assured of winning my final major, where one of my rewards is eternal life in heaven with you. In Jesus's name, amen.

GOLF 30

Missed Opportunities? Refocus!

Luke 9:62, Acts 20–24, 1 Corinthians 9:22

Life is worth nothing unless I use it for doing the
work assigned me by the Lord Jesus, the work of
telling others the Good News about God's mighty
kindness and love.

—Acts 20:24 (TLB)

Although I had been a Christian for almost five years, I
missed some opportunities one summer when I got con-
sumed by golf. I made my first hole in one, and two weeks
later, I matched my best golf round ever when I shot 65
with a ball in the water. Hey, I found the secret. Visions of
the Champions Tour paraded in my head.

I proceeded to hit several thousand balls on the practice
tee over the next month, and I ignored God leading me
to have open gym in order to play more golf. I reassured
myself, "It won't matter. The boys won't miss it." I believe
that God noticed. Luke 9:62 says, "Jesus told him, 'Anyone
who allows himself to be distracted from the work that I
plan for him is not fit for the kingdom of God.'"

Later that summer, I partially tore a tendon in my left elbow and had painful tendonitis for six months. I was amazed how often that pain in my elbow reminded me of where I should have been spending more of my time. But during my down time, I got in touch with God's plan through the youth sports ministry at my church. I believe that God's plan is for me to use my passion for sports to help reach someone who could miss spending eternity with him. That's one reason that I wrote this book.

When was the last time that you cried for someone who is unsaved? If you're a Christian and you envision a family member or friend spending eternity separated from God, it should bring you to tears. Evangelist Charles Spurgeon once issued this challenge: "Have you no wish for others to be saved? Then you are not saved yourself. Be sure of that." Paul said in Acts 20:24, "Life is worth nothing unless I use it for doing the work assigned me by the Lord Jesus, the work of telling others the good news about God's mighty kindness and love!" John Wesley, the founder of the Methodist Church, stated, "You have nothing to do but to save souls. Therefore spend and be spent in this work."

If you feel lukewarm for Jesus, pray now that God will rekindle your heart for the unsaved and reach out to your lost friends. If you are not sure how to share, you can always ask a Christian brother or sister for guidance.

Prayer: Dear Father God, may I realize that nothing is as important as reaching the lost. Help me recognize and take advantage of the opportunities you give me to share Christ with my friends in words, deeds, and actions. In Jesus's holy name, amen.

GOLF 31

Is It Just Luck?

Ask and you will receive, seek and you will find,
knock and the door will be opened to you.

—Matthew 7:7

The par-3 twelfth hole at Augusta is one of the most nerve-racking holes in golf. Only 155 yards long across Rae's Creek, the narrow green is positioned diagonally to the right, and the steep bank slopes dangerously toward the water. When the wind swirls, it's very hard to detect which way it is blowing. Short right is in the water, long left is up in the foliage on the hill. Many Masters have been lost at this dangerous hole.

One year, the Thursday round was interrupted by weather. Play began on Friday at 7:30 a.m. to complete the first round. Jack Nicklaus had only played ten holes on Thursday, and being the big Jack fan that I was, I talked my brother, LE, into getting up at 4:30 a.m. and meeting me in Augusta at 7:00 a.m. We needed thirty minutes to walk to Amen Corner, the farthest point on the course, to see Jack Nicklaus complete his first round.

When the weather is cold in the early morning, golfers have trouble staying loose. When you are tight, you miss shots to the right. On a clear but chilly forty-degree morning, Jack pushed his opening tee shot on eleven to the right and missed the green to the right with his approach but managed to chip close and get his par. When he came to the twelfth tee, there couldn't have been more than a dozen people down there to watch the four-time Masters champion. I was within five yards of Jack. The flagstick was on the right edge, the most dangerous hole placement. I could see Jack aiming for the center of the green to play safe, but he blocked his tee shot. He had enough club though, and the ball finished six feet from the hole.

Everyone applauded, and the guy next to me yelled, "Great shot, Jack!"

Under my breath, I muttered to him, "But he wasn't aiming there."

Jack heard me, turned around, and said with a wry smile, "You're right about that!"

In 1992, Masters champion Fred Couples hit his tee shot on the twelfth hole short to the right. The ball landed on the steep bank, which was wet from overnight rain, somehow grew teeth, and didn't roll back into the water. He made a par and won by two shots.

Sometimes we receive unexpected blessings and don't even realize they came from God. Certainly, Jack and Fred were blessed with fortunate breaks on these shots, but oftentimes, when we get a blessing from God, we call it good fortune, good luck, or a small world. There is nothing small about God's world.

Once I was obedient with a couple of small things that I had been struggling with. Afterward, I felt peace about the situation and thanked God for the special blessing that I believe that he sent my way. Do our good fortunes happen by chance? I don't think so. Not when blessings come from a God who put the entire universe together in six days.

Prayer: Father God, sometimes I am not sure if it is you that just blessed my life. May I improve my discernment so that when you send a blessing my way, I see it and give you immediate thanks. In Jesus's name, I pray. Amen.

GOLF 32

Use That Fifteenth Club in Your Bag

Romans 8:26; Acts 1:8; Ephesians 4:30, 6:10

Be strong in the Lord, and in his great power!

—Ephesians 6:10

From 1992 through 1994, Ben Crenshaw's game had been deteriorating as he slipped farther down the money list. To list him as a serious contender for the Masters green jacket in 1995 would have been purely a sentimental choice, even for his most ardent supporters. On Monday night of Masters week, Ben received distressing news that his long-time coach, Harvey Penick, had passed away in Austin, Texas. Crenshaw and his close friend, Tom Kite, who was another Penick student, flew from Augusta to Austin for Harvey's memorial service. Ben arrived back in Augusta on Wednesday night, obviously feeling a deep sense of loss.

Working with his veteran caddie, Carl Jackson, Ben found a swing key on the range before his Thursday round. After three days of driving the ball consistently and making his usual bushel basket of putts, Ben found himself in contention on Sunday. He so desperately wanted to win the tournament in memory of Harvey Penick that he could have allowed his emotions to get the best of him.

However, Gentle Ben fired a great final round and left himself the luxury of being able to make bogey on the last hole. After cleaning up a one-foot putt, he buried his face in his hands and wept uncontrollably as Carl gave him a hug.

After the green jacket ceremony, Ben spoke of the peace that he felt during the madness of a frantic Augusta back-nine finish. Crenshaw was quoted that he felt like Harvey was there with him during the round and how that memory gave him strength, almost like having a fifteenth club in his bag. Perhaps the spirit of Harvey Penick was right there with Ben, whispering in Ben's ear to take dead aim. It was one of the great final round finishes in Masters history.

You and I have a fifteenth club in our bags that we rarely use, and that is the power of the Holy Spirit. Recall that Jesus said to the disciples just before he ascended into heaven that they will receive the power of the Holy Spirit and that they will be witnesses to him in Jerusalem and in all Judea and Samaria and to the ends of the earth (Acts 1:8). The Holy Spirit resides within us to help us with our daily problems, just as Harvey's memory kept Ben focused. Let's take advantage of the power of the Holy Spirit, which God sealed us with at our redemption (Ephesians 4:30). In times of turmoil and stress, let's be strong in the Lord and in his great power (Ephesians 6:10).

Prayer: Dear Heavenly Father, may I remember that I have the power of the Holy Spirit within me to do great things for your kingdom. May you receive every bit of the glory. In Jesus's name, amen.

GOLF 33

Go for It Like Arnie!

Preach the Word of God urgently at all times,
whenever you get the chance, in season and out,
when it is convenient and when it is not.

—2 Timothy 4:2

Arnold Palmer is considered by many golf experts to be the most popular golfer to ever play the game. His passionate, swashbuckling, go-for-broke style endeared him to legions of fans for over fifty years. So popular was Arnie during his heyday that he remains a beloved icon.

Arnold won eight major championships, including four Masters titles. Augusta is where Arnold took the game of golf to another level as TV aired his dramatic win in 1960 when he birdied the last two holes to win his second green jacket. The popularity of golf and the rich purses in professional golf have their roots in Arnie's success at Augusta.

Arnold had powerful blacksmith arms and swung at the ball with all of his might with a club-twirling finish. He played out of trouble quite often and hit some amazing recovery shots that wowed his followers, called Arnie's Army. Sometimes it worked out, and sometimes it didn't, but Arnie played with a passion for the game and never backed off.

Leading the final round of the 1964 Masters by a comfortable six shots, Arnie went for the green in two on the par-5 fifteenth hole with a mighty smash of a 3-wood and tore a huge divot out of the fairway. Squinting into the sun, Arnie said, "Did it get over [the water in front of the green]? Did it make it?"

His playing competitor Dave Marr deadpanned, "Arnold, your divot got over."

What can Christians learn from the legend of Arnold Palmer? First of all, Arnie had incredible charisma and an engaging smile. He was incredibly gracious with everyone that he met. He constantly made eye contact and shook hands with the gallery. According to some, he could make a complete stranger feel like a longtime friend. But most of all, we can learn from the passion with which he tackled the game of golf. God doesn't want a bunch of wimpy Christians. He wants believers to witness for Christ with passion. If we witnessed for Christ with a passion equal to that displayed by Arnie in his workplace, the kingdom around the world would grow much more quickly and the second coming of Jesus would happen much sooner. Paul taught us to "Go for it!" when he urged believers to share Christ urgently at two times: when it is convenient and when it is not.

Prayer: Father God, may I tap the passion with which Arnie played the game of golf and Paul preached your gospel. May I hang with people who have a passion for living and a passion for reaching others for Christ. In Jesus's name, amen.

GOLF 34

Single-Minded Focus

Preach the Word of God urgently at all times,
whenever you get the chance, in season and out,
when it is convenient and when it is not.

—2 Timothy 4:2

Some golfers are legendary for their ability to focus on the task at hand. When Nicklaus needed to hole a putt, he would crouch over the ball for what seemed like an eternity. Then, once he was absolutely sure that he had the line down, he would stroke the putt and invariably find the bottom of the cup, particularly if the putt was a big one. Who can forget the forty-footer he holed in the 1975 Masters as he leaped around the green with his putter thrust high into the air as a disconsolate Tom Weiskopf watched from the sixteenth tee. Then there is the 1986 Masters seventeenth hole, the replay we've seen a million times when Jack holes the putt to take the lead and Verne Lundquist shouts, "Yes, sir!"

Perhaps no golfer had more of a reputation for possessing steely concentration than Ben Hogan. Affectionately nicknamed the Wee Ice Mon by the Scots after his 1953

British Open triumph at Carnoustie, Hogan rarely spoke during a competitive round because he was so into his game. At the 1947 Masters, his playing partner, Claude Harmon, made an ace, a hole in one, on the treacherous twelfth hole. Hogan made a deuce by holing a birdie putt. When Hogan reached the thirteenth tee, he asked Harmon, "What did you make?"

If there was any apostle that had Hogan's steely focus in golf, it had to be Paul. Look what Paul endured yet remained steadfast in his desire to see the Jews and the Gentiles of his day come to a personal relationship with the Savior that Paul had once persecuted. If we simply live with an eternal focus each day, whether or not it rivals Paul's focus or Hogan's on the links, we will be much more prepared to spread the good news of the gospel of Jesus Christ.

Prayer: Dear Father, I thank you for the amazing Apostle Paul and what I can learn from his passion for sharing the gospel each day. May I have a daily awareness of eternity and the opportunities that you place in front of us each day. In Jesus's name, amen.

GOLF 35

Need a Mulligan?

> For whosoever shall call upon the name of the
> Lord shall be saved.
>
> —Romans 10:13 (KJV)

It is a fairly common practice on some American golf courses that businessmen will rush to the first tee without a warm-up and take two and pick the best drive. Take two refers to the first tee ball and a second tee ball called a mulligan.

There is a story about an American who played the Old Course at St. Andrews, Scotland, for the first time. As he reached for his second ball, the caddie said, "You will now be playing your third shot." The American got the hint, picked up his tee, and played his first ball.

In 2008, with the help of many friends from church, I founded the Golf for His Glory tournament that benefited our youth, missions, and ministries at Mt. Zion UMC and served as an evangelistic outreach to share the gospel of Jesus Christ. As I sought ways to share the good news of Christ with the 115 golfers who played the first year, my good friend, Robert, introduced me to Pocket Power

Testaments. This booklet of the gospel of John includes commentary that comes in a variety of themes, including golf. On the cover is a picture of a golf ball in the woods in thick grass behind a tree, and the caption reads, "Do You Need a Mulligan?" *Very clever*, I thought, and most of the golfers seemed to enjoy the gift of the gospel of John.

Do you ever feel sometimes that you just don't have a lot going for you? It's easy to get frustrated when things aren't going well. Perhaps you are feeling the burden of expectations or your family is struggling financially or emotionally. Have you continued to struggle to do it by yourself? Right now, do you feel that you are four down with four to play? If this situation describes you, have you looked up to the Ultimate Caddy and said, "God, I can't do this by myself anymore. I desperately need a mulligan, a second chance. Can you please send me Jesus?" How would it feel to know the peace that passes understanding? If you turn from your self-centered ways and confess Christ as your Savior, not only will you receive eternal life, but you're on your way to finding the peace that comes from knowing that this world is not all there is. You get the mulligan of all time when you receive Christ. The Holy Spirit will help you with your daily problems and help you pray when you ache and can't possibly put your thoughts into words.

⛳

Prayer: Father God, thank you for the clean, fresh start from our selfish efforts that always leave us wanting more than this life has to offer. Jesus Christ, your Son, is the mulligan each one of us needs at some point in our lives. Thank you for the saving grace that is available through Jesus. In his holy name, I pray. Amen.

GOLF 36

How Should Christians React to Tiger?

If your brother trespass against you, rebuke him;
and if he repent, forgive him. And if he trespass
against you seven times in a day, and seven times in
a day turn again to you, saying, I repent; you shall
forgive him.

—Luke 17:3–4(KJV)

Everyone in the world of golf had their eyes on Tiger Woods at Augusta National Golf Club in April 2010. Tiger returned from a self-imposed exile from the PGA Tour after he admitted sexual misconduct and impropriety. Certainly there were mixed reactions to Tiger's return, but generally the galleries treated him like any other player. Certainly there was not the adulation to which he had grown accustomed. Upon his return, most golf fans wanted him to be gracious to the galleries, like Arnie and Jack and Phil had been, and to exhibit better self-control when his tee shot went wayward.

In 2009 Kenny Perry, at the age of forty-nine, was a yipped chip from being the oldest man to win the Masters. Certainly he has enough game to put on that green jacket. However, Kenny made a statement without his golf clubs.

He put someone else ahead of himself in a demonstration of Christian love and brotherhood. Kenny told the Masters committee that he would play with Tiger the first two days of the 2010 Masters. He felt empathy for the man even though Tiger let his family, a lot of kids, and the golfing world down. You couldn't expect other golfers to follow Kenny's lead. Obviously, they didn't want to get caught up in the circus and hurt their games and the only chance some might ever have to win a Masters.

Regarding Tiger's situation, let's leave the judgment to God. He has proven that he is perfectly capable of judging all of us. There has not been nor will there be a sin that God cannot forgive when someone comes with a repentant heart. Neither should there be one that we cannot forgive. Forgive your brother seventy times seven (Matthew 18:22).

Recall the example of Jesus drawing in the dirt to take the icy stares away from the adulterous woman. The Pharisees sought to stone the woman for her sins, but Jesus said, "Let him who is without sin cast the first stone" (John 8:7). The eldest Pharisee dropped his stone and walked away. The others followed suit until only Jesus and the grateful woman remained. Jesus told her to go and sin no more.

Surely Tiger appreciated anything his playing partners and the galleries did to help make him feel welcome.

Prayer: Dear Father, it's easy to take potshots at people who have committed worse sins than I have. Or have they? Help me realize that sin is sin in your eyes and that I need to keep my house clean through frequent confession of my sins, and thank you for your wonderful forgiveness. In Jesus's name, amen.

GOLF 37

Ryder Cup Magic at Brookline

Mark 9:34, Acts 1:8, 26; Hebrews 11:1, 6

What is faith? Faith is the confident assurance that
something you want is going to happen.

—Hebrews 11:1 (TLB)

Every two years, the best twelve golfers from the United
States and the best twelve from the European continent
compete in an intense three-day competition called the
Ryder Cup, which was named after the founder of the
competition, Samuel Ryder, in 1927. The competition
thrills golf fans around the world, and it gives players who
are accustomed to competing for individual honors, money,
and titles, the chance to win or lose as a team.

On the eve of the Sunday singles final at Brookline
Country Club in the 1999 Ryder Cup, the Americans trailed
10–6 and had been roundly criticized by the American press
for being a disparate group of individuals. The American
captain, Ben Crenshaw, saw something in his team that the
media experts were not seeing. At the press conference fol-
lowing the matches on Saturday, Crenshaw pointed to the

media and said, "I'm a big believer in fate. I have a good feeling about tomorrow. That's all I'm gonna say."

You might or might not believe in fate, but certainly Captain Crenshaw had faith in his team. Despite the fact that no team had ever erased a four-point margin on Sunday, he had a confident assurance (see Hebrews 11:1) that they would come through in the clutch. Crenshaw still believed his individual stars would come together as a twelve-man team.

In a brilliant strategic move on Sunday, Crenshaw front-loaded his lineup and put his top six golfers out first in the singles matches. Roars erupted all over the course as the Americans quickly made up lost ground by winning the first six singles matches, followed by Justin Leonard's forty-five-foot bomb on the seventeenth hole. Leonard's putt won the Ryder Cup for the Americans and had Crenshaw on his knees kissing Mother Earth. Ben kept the faith in his team.

Near the time of Jesus's crucifixion, after almost three years of following Jesus, seeing the miracles, and hearing the message, remember how the disciples argued with each other about who was the greatest (Mark 9:34)? It was still all about individuals. Judas Iscariot would soon betray Jesus. When Christ was led to the cross, the eleven remaining disciples, except John, scattered like a covey of quail.

But Christ kept the faith in them. After all, the future of Christianity rested in the hands of these eleven average human beings. Matthias was selected to replace Judas Iscariot (Acts 1:26) as the twelfth disciple. After Jesus ascended into heaven, that average group of individuals received the Holy Spirit as Jesus had promised (Acts 1:8). Collectively, they became the most important twelve-man team the world has ever known.

Prayer: Most wonderful Father God, when I look at all that the twelve disciples were able to accomplish, I am in awe that you would trust them with the future of the world. Please entrust me to do the small things that can further the kingdom. In Jesus's holy name, I pray. Amen.

GOLF 38

My Round at Augusta: What I Learned

He is always watching everything that concerns us.

—1 Peter 5:7

It was the first full weekend of 1974. I had gone to Augusta with my roommate, Tim, to play golf for the weekend. On Friday night, I called my friend, Bob, to see how he was doing. I had played college golf with Bob the previous year, and he had gotten married and landed a dream position at Augusta National. When he invited us to come play on Saturday, I couldn't believe it. I was going to play Augusta National! I could hardly sleep, given my anticipation.

What a thrill to drive down Magnolia Lane in Fulcher's 1967 Chevy! The caddies met us in the parking lot on a dreary, drizzly, forty-five-degree day. We teed off around noon, and my first tee shot went straight down the middle. I had a decent front nine, and having a caddy read the greens and make my club selections really helped.

Unfortunately, the wheels started to come off. I bogeyed ten and eleven and hit in the water on the tough par-3 twelfth. I laid up for my third shot on the par-5 thirteenth, and my caddy suggested a pitching wedge. I had a bit of a side hill lie and had hit my last shot fat. I hesitated and asked him for a 9-iron, which I smoked over the green for another bogey. That was the last piece of advice that I received that afternoon.

I should have taken his advice. My caddy had many years of experience and knew my distances by the second hole. I should have listened to him instead of being hard-headed and hitting a different club. Even though my caddy offered no more advice, he still walked beside me and carried my clubs.

We would be smart to take God's advice. After all, God knew us before he knit us, and he invented time. So that's a lot of experience right there. When we become self-centered and stop taking God's advice, he can go silent on us for a time. He might leave us alone for a season, but he will not abandon us because he will come back for his children. If we shout out for his help, he is only a single prayer away. No matter the situation, God loves us and will always pull the right club for us.

⛳

Prayer: Father God, may I seek your guidance so that I pull the right club much more often than trying to do things on my own. Thank you that you love me so much and that you are always there when I need to talk to you. In Jesus's name, amen.

GOLF 39

My Most Painful Day on the Golf Course

> Surely He has borne our griefs,
> and carried our sorrows.
>
> —Isaiah 53:4

It was the final round of the 1974 Georgia Junior College State Tournament at the University of Georgia golf course. My team from Middle Georgia College was right in the thick of it to win it all. I turned the front side in thirty-eight after hitting eight of nine greens on a tough golf course. But I slipped up with bogeys on two relatively easy par 4s and came to the par-5 twelfth hole. After a bombed drive, I was in position to hit the peninsula green in two for a sure birdie and a possible eagle. I lined up my 3-iron carefully and gave it all that I had. I flushed it, and the ball flew high in the air on a line just left of the flagstick.

That's when the nightmare occurred. The ball landed no more than thirty feet from the front right pin placement. Instead of bounding onto the green, the ball caught the top of the bank and fell back into the water. I made double bogey on my way to an inglorious 43 on the back nine. We lost the state title by only two shots, which meant that if I had simply shot 40 on the back side, the title would have been ours. I was crestfallen and felt that I was the one who cost us the state title.

That shot happened over forty years ago, and I still have the same vision of my ball hitting the bank and toppling into the water. What I would have given at the time for that ball to make the green. A birdie would have renewed my confidence, and who knows what would have happened. It was the most disappointing and painful day on the golf course that I ever had.

God hurts when we hurt. Jesus Christ came to this earth from heaven so that he could know exactly how we feel, no matter the disappointment or the pain. When we feel like we've hit rock bottom in a relationship or in school or in a job or in a sporting event, we can rest assured that Jesus has felt any emotion that we could possibly feel. Through Christ, we can find solace in our disappointments and failures.

Prayer: Father God, I appreciate you sending Jesus so that he could know what it's like to hurt when we hurt. When I feel so low, help me remember that Jesus felt depths I could never imagine. Thank you for always caring and watching everything that concerns me. In Jesus's name, amen.

GOLF 40

The Keys to Victory

Romans 7:7–9

I had not known sin, but by the Law.

—Romans 7:7 (KJV)

At most major golf tournaments, particularly the US Open, the champion invariably excels in three key statistical areas. First, the winner must drive the golf ball into the fairway the majority of the time. The Open rough is so deep and wiry that stray tee shots often lead to bogeys. Second, the winner must be at or near the lead for the week in hitting greens in regulation. Once the player is on the green, he needs to get down in two putts, which is the regulation number for a par. If any of these facets of the game is off, it will place so much pressure on the player's other facets that any chance of winning will disappear. Rory McIlroy, the 2011 US Open winner, drove the ball long and straight, led the field in greens in regulation, and three-putted only once on his way to a stunning eight-shot victory!

Just as the US Open places golfers under tremendous pressure, the devil constantly keeps the pressure on you to keep you from a relationship with Jesus Christ. You can win that battle and come to know Christ by executing the three keys to victory in Jesus.

The first key is that you must come to the realization that you need to exchange your sinful and self-centered life for a selfless one devoted to Christ. When you achieve that realization, confess your sins to God and vow to turn away from sin and turn toward him going forward. God will honor your confession and cleanse you of all the sins you have ever committed. What amazing news it is that you can be freed from the tyranny of sin that plagued you for your entire life!

The second key is to trust that Jesus Christ died for your sins on the cross and that through his blood it is possible to go to heaven. Trust means believing with all your heart, mind, and soul that Jesus is your Savior and Lord.

Once you have committed to live your life to Christ, the third key is to practice the following spiritual disciplines to grow as a disciple of Jesus Christ. Be obedient to God by reading your Bible daily and praying, which is simply talking to God and listening for his inner voice to guide you. Obedience to God also includes attending worship services each Sunday and hanging with other believers to learn from each other.

Prayer: Father God, thank you for so clearly giving me the keys to victory in Jesus. May I love you with my whole heart and be obedient to you each day. Thank you for loving me unconditionally and more than I can understand and deserve as a sinner. In Jesus's precious name, amen.

Take More Club

Acts 1:8, Romans 8:26

You shall receive power when the Holy Spirit
comes upon you.

—Acts 1:8

The most common mistake that most golfers make is to try to hit the ball too hard into a strong wind. A strong wind against you will magnify the margin of error of your shot, and your mind plays tricks on you. You think, I can swing 10 percent harder and hit it 10 percent farther. But what happens is that when you grip the club tighter, trying to hit it farther, your big muscles tighten because you are not as confident, and you get off your natural rhythm. The result is usually a mishit shot that falls short and right of the green into the bunker or the water hazard.

What is the key to playing a shot into a strong wind? Take one or two more clubs. Instead of taking a 7-iron, use a less-lofted club such as a 6-iron or even a 5-iron. Swinging easier with a less-lofted club allows you to swing smoother and keep the ball under the wind. The extra power of the less-lofted club propels your ball where it needs to go. Tap the power of the stronger club when you're going against the wind.

Often we try to do it by ourselves in our personal lives. We believe that we can force the action by just trying harder or by cramming more activities, more e-mails, and more calls into our day. But when we try 10 percent harder, it doesn't always produce better results. Sometimes our extra effort is counterproductive, and we can actually cause ourselves more problems.

We believers often neglect the Holy Spirit, the Person who lives within us. This is the same Holy Spirit that Jesus promised the disciples that came upon them on the day of Pentecost. Talk about going into a strong headwind. How could twelve ordinary, flawed individuals have changed the world with their strength alone? Their efforts would have been futile. When our efforts are futile or we feel overwhelmed, we need to tap into the awesome power of the Holy Spirit. The first phrase in Romans 8:26 tells us, "The Holy Spirit helps us with our daily problems." When we consistently invite God to be present throughout our day, God gives us the extra power we need to overcome obstacles through the presence of the Holy Spirit.

⌐

Prayer: Father and Most Holy God, may I realize that just gritting my teeth harder and climbing into a bunker mentality mode are not the answer. May I step back and take the time to bring you into the decision-making process when I face difficulties. In Jesus's name, amen.

GOLF 42

Make It Look Easy

But God demonstrates His own love toward us, in that while we were still sinners, Christ died for us.

—Romans 5:8

Watch the pros on the practice range at the Masters or other major golf tournaments. There are hundreds of years of collective experience there, and a ton of sweat equity went into honing the skills of their craft. We marvel as we watch the repetitive ease with which these men power the golf balls three hundred plus yards and hit irons so accurately with so little effort. Their skills around the green as they strike precise chip shots, amazing bunker shots, and pressure putts leave us shaking our heads in wonderment. When we compare their swings to our uncoordinated efforts, it is evident why we struggle to shoot anywhere close to par.

Speaking of repetitive ease, at the Masters in 1973, the players would hit their personal practice balls on the range. Their caddies would stand 150 to 200 yards away and catch the soaring iron shots on one hop and place the balls in the bag.

Once, Lee Trevino hit irons one after another just perfect, and a woman gushed in awe behind him, "Oh, that is beautiful! How amazing!" Trevino finally turned to her and teasingly said, "Lady, what do you expect from the US Open champion, ground balls?"

The pros make it look easy because it cost them so many thousands of hours of practice to get them where they need to be. God made our salvation easy because it cost him so much when he sent Jesus Christ to the cross to die for our sins. No matter how much sweat equity we put into good deeds trying to earn our way into heaven, it will never work because it was by grace that we have been saved through faith. By placing his Son on the cross, it was as if God played this incredible round of golf and left us with only having to make a straight-in two-footer up the hill. It's right there for the taking if only we will pull the putter out of the bag and finish it off by repenting of our sin and confessing Christ as our Savior and Lord.

🚩

Prayer: Most holy and gracious God, I can never fathom the amount of effort, blood, sweat, and tears that Jesus undertook for me so that I could have an easy way to heaven. Thank you for your unending love for me. In Jesus's name, amen.

GOLF 43

God Has No Waiting List

I am The Way, The Truth, and The Life.

—John 14:6

As the Masters rolls around each year, I get a slightly sinking feeling occasionally when someone brings up how hard it is to get badges to the Masters. I have been so fortunate since 1973 to use the badges that my aunt and uncle first purchased in the 1950s. In the 1970s, Augusta National Golf Club closed the waiting list because there were thousands of people who wanted badges, and so few badges became available. So I didn't bother to pursue the waiting list. I had the false assurance that the badges would always be there.

But I cringed when I heard a story of a person who had been on the waiting list for twenty-one years and finally received badges in 2010. I did the math. Let's see. He got on the wait list in 1989. I could have been on it years before and didn't bother. What was I thinking? All it would have taken is several minutes to write a letter to Augusta National and a thirty-seven-cent stamp. Don't get me wrong. I am grateful to have attended over thirty Masters tournaments.

But I knew the situation, had the knowledge, and didn't act on it. So mentally, I give myself a kick because they could have been used by me, my daughters, and my wife.

In some ways, that can be similar to the unwillingness of people to heed the warning that there is only one way to heaven. The only way is by confessing our sins, which is called repentance, and placing our faith in Jesus Christ as Savior and Lord. Perhaps you hear the story of a person who received Christ later in life and you say to yourself, *I need to get around to doing that one day.* But you can't come to Christ when you want to. You must be drawn by the Holy Spirit. Mentally, you will give yourself a kick when you eventually make the decision. *What was I thinking? Why didn't I do that earlier?* All it takes is a few minutes for a confession of your sins to God and asking Jesus to be at the center of your life. You know the situation, and you have the knowledge, but you haven't acted on it. What about now?

Now here's the difference in the Masters' wait list and God's list. On God's list, you don't have to wait for somebody to come off. You can leapfrog everybody on the list and come immediately into God's family because of his free gift of grace through faith in Jesus Christ. No wait list for eternal life, the greatest gift of all time.

Prayer: Father God, I thank you that you have no wait list to come to know Christ and become a believer. You also have no unreachable list. Help me remember to pray for those who are still waiting to come to Christ. In Jesus's name, amen.

GOLF 44

The Big Three

Matthew 17:1–2, Mark 5:37, 14:33

And He took Peter and James and John with Him.

—Mark 14:33

Arnold Palmer, Jack Nicklaus, and Gary Player were called the Big Three because they were the three dominant golfers of the 1960s. These three Hall of Famers won nine consecutive Masters from 1958 through 1966. Fans of the era enjoyed seeing them play so much that eighteen-hole made-for-TV showdowns were created, which made them even more famous. The show was called *Big Three Golf.*

Palmer, Nicklaus, and Player were distinctly different golfers and personalities. Arnold was the most popular with the fans because of his big strong forearms, swashbuckling persona, and go-for-broke style. Palmer oozed charisma like few athletes in sports. In 1963, the Masters limited ticket sales for the first time. Why? It was due to Arnie's popularity.

Jack was the big kid with a crew cut from Ohio seeking to dethrone Palmer as the best player in the game. Despite incurring the wrath of some fans that were jealous of him overtaking Palmer, Jack eventually won the fans over with his big booming drives, towering irons, and deft putting.

Gary was the little South African, much smaller than the two giants of the game but the first physical fitness fanatic among golfers. Player used his scrappy, bulldog determination to win two Masters titles during this time.

Since that time, there have been dominant golfers, but none went head-to-head for a decade as these three golfers did. During their illustrious careers, Nicklaus, Palmer, and Player won thirty-five major championships.

Peter, James, and John were the big three disciples for Jesus, who took them along for his majors like the raising of a girl from the dead, the transfiguration, and the garden of Gethsemane. Their personalities were certainly different. Peter emerged as the leader among the disciples but was often headstrong and had conflicting ideas about how Jesus ought to do things. Yet Jesus told Peter that he would be the rock upon which his church would be built, and Peter became a key leader in the early church. James and John were fishermen and brothers, James being the older. They once argued who should sit at the right and left hand of Jesus, and this debate infuriated the other disciples. For this and other similar acts, the two were nicknamed sons of thunder. But their bravery could not be questioned in the end.

Prayer: Father God, thank you for the early disciples and for the contributions of the Big Three. Even though they didn't always get it, their record improved after the Holy Spirit came to reside in them. For their courage and loyalty to Jesus, we give you thanks. In Jesus's name, amen.

GOLF 45

Masters Qualification

Matthew 10:32–33, John 14:6

Whosoever acknowledges Me before others, I will
also acknowledge before my Father in heaven.

—Matthew 10:32

Every spectator at the Masters is given a spectator's guide,
which shows you how to get around the course and provides
profiles of each golfer. In each profile, there is one number
or multiple numbers to the right of the player's name. The
numbers are codes that indicate how the player qualified
for the Masters. In fact, there were eighteen different ways
that a golfer could earn a trip to the 2010 Masters. Some of
the qualifications include being a past Masters champion,
finishing in the top eight at the 2009 US Open, finishing
in the top fifty in the world golf rankings, and winning a
PGA tournament since the 2009 Masters. In 2010, Phil
Mickelson met nine of the eighteen qualifications.

Some folks are under the mistaken impression that
there are at least eighteen ways to get into heaven. Those
fallacies include the following:

"I've been good enough to make the cut."

"I'm no adulterer or murderer."

"God is not the kind of God who would keep me out of heaven. He's a loving God."

"I make the cut compared to my friends, who are much worse than me."

"Look at all the ways I've helped people. Surely that counts for something."

Jesus made it abundantly clear that there is only one qualification that will ever enable you to see the true Masters, God and Jesus, in heaven. Jesus said, "I am the Way, the Truth, and the Life. No one comes to the Father except through me." You cannot earn the grace of God, which is free to all who turn from sin and confess that Jesus Christ is Lord.

Prayer: Most holy and magnificent God, may I be ever aware when my friends and family members believe there is more than one way to the Father. Help me share your good news in ways that they will truly understand what it takes to see the Masters in heaven. In Jesus's name, amen.

GOLF 46

Got an Amen Corner?

Matthew 26:34–49

Sit here while I go and pray over there.

—Matthew 26:36

Even at ninety-eight years old, my dad could still recount stories from his youth in North Alabama. It is amazing to think that he knew people who lived during the Civil War, and yet here he is, living in the age of blogs and Twitter in the twenty-first century. One of my favorite stories is about the amen corner of his boyhood church. He told me that the women and children would sit in the center pews in front of the preacher, and the men folk would sit on the side pews. When the preacher made a good point as judged by one of the men, the man would say, "Amen." Dad said that the louder the men said, "Amen," the louder the preacher would get, feeding off the congregation.

Another type of amen corner was named in 1958 by Herbert Warren Wind, the famous golf historian and writer. Amen Corner at the Augusta National Golf Club consisted of the dangerous second shot to the eleventh green, the par-3 twelfth, and the daring drive on thirteen with Rae's Creek lurking to the left. Seeking to capture the excitement of Palmer's first Masters win in 1958 where Amen Corner played such a huge role, Wind made reference in his Masters article to "Shouting in the Amen Corner," a popular big band jazz tune.

According to Masters.org, Palmer embedded his tee shot in mud on the twelfth hole in the final round. He was allowed by the rules official to play two balls, the original ball with which he made a double bogey, and a second ball as a free drop with which he made a par. Palmer eagled the thirteenth hole, and when he was on the fifteenth hole, word came that his free drop had been honored. Immediately, he took the lead and held on for his green jacket.

There is another type of amen corner that each of us needs. It is that quiet corner or place that each believer should go to start each day with God. My time consists of a couple of devotionals, including *My Utmost for His Highest*, prayer time, and meditation. In the solitude of the early morning, so often God speaks to us through quiet utterances in our minds. My amen corner has varied from place to place, but my recent amen corner is the corner of our sofa in the living room.

It is with even more certainty that you can meet God in your amen corner compared to seeing the top golfers in the world at Augusta National's Amen Corner each April. How can I be so sure? Because Augusta National became a pasture for four years during World War II. God didn't take days off from anyone's amen corner during that time.

Prayer: Father God, most precious Lord, may I realize that the precious time that I spend with you each day in my amen corner keeps me from making bogeys and double bogeys during my day. Thank you for the blessing and the privilege to make a tee time with you any time that I wish. In Jesus's name, amen.

GOLF 47

Practice Before You Play

This Book of the Law shall not depart from your
mouth, but you shall meditate in it day and night.

—Joshua 1:8

The brand-new Masters practice range built in 2010 was
incredible to see. It was built on top of the gravel parking
lot that had been adjacent to the first hole for more than
fifty years. One pro said that he just wanted to stay there
and practice. Pros could practice shaping their drives left to
right and right to left because trees lined pretend fairways
out on the range. The vast semicircular tee box was several
hundred yards long and allowed the pros to practice shots
against any type of wind. For jaded professional golfers to
be giddy over a practice range when they had seen hun-
dreds before, it was obviously quite special.

Typically, a golfer competing in the Masters will go
through a standard warm-up routine. The golfer will
stretch his muscles and hit numerous short wedges to find
his rhythm. Soft wedges are followed by short irons, middle
irons, long irons, metal woods, and finally, the driver. The
ball-striking practice is followed by many chips, pitches,

bunker shots, and putts before moving to the first tee to begin the round.

A top golfer warms up thoroughly before each round. With that preparation, the pro ensures he will be fully prepared for each shot, saving himself several strokes on each round. If a particular club gives him grief during the round, then the pro will spend extra time after the round addressing that particular flaw.

As believers, we would be well served to get into that type of routine before and after the activities of our day. The practice range or warm-up for the believer is with a devotion that is taken in a quiet place. Scripture reading is geared to that devotion, prayer, and meditation. Without that preparation, our day simply will not go as well as it could have. By spending extra quiet time in the morning, we save ourselves several headaches each day and ensure that we will be prepared for the shots that Satan takes at us. If a particular problem surfaces during the day such as anger, impatience, or greed, that problem can be addressed by specific Scripture study before we retire for the evening. Groundwork in the morning, followed by specifics in the evening, is a winning combination that will help you play many par and sub-par "rounds" for him during your lifetime.

Prayer: Father God, help me spend time with you in the Word each morning to prepare for my day, just as a golf pro at the Masters spends time on the practice range before playing his round. Grant me the discipline to maintain good daily habits. In Jesus's name, amen.

GOLF 48

Arnie, You Don't Have a Chance

John 3:16–17

God did not send His Son into the world to
condemn it, but to save it.

—John 3:17

After the third round of the 1960 US Open at Cherry Hills Golf Club in Denver, Colorado, Arnold Palmer trailed by seven shots with a total of 215. As he glumly ate a sandwich before going out for the afternoon round to complete thirty-six holes on the final day, he asked his sportswriter friend, Bob Drum, of the *Pittsburgh Post-Gazette*, what it would take to win the tournament. The Drummer told him that 280 wins the Open, and he implied that Palmer didn't have it in him to shoot a 65 and, therefore, didn't have a chance to win. Clearly miffed, Palmer finished his sandwich and stormed out of the clubhouse.

It might have been a psychological ploy to fire him up. Palmer threw caution to the wind and hit driver on the tight first hole instead of the iron he had laid up with the first three rounds. He burned a low scorcher through the rough up onto the first green almost 350 yards away. That was the first of six birdies that Arnie would make. With each birdie, his gallery grew larger, and word of the charge that Arnie was so famous for swept back to the clubhouse. When an out-of-breath Drum made his way to the ninth tee, Arnie saw him and smirked, as if to say, *No chance? I'll show you!* Palmer shot 65 and won the Open by two shots over a young phenom named Jack Nicklaus and a fading superstar named Ben Hogan. Great stuff.

Speaking of Nicklaus, in 1986, the late Tom McCollister handicapped the Masters field in the *Atlanta Journal-Constitution* the prior Sunday and essentially wrote that Jack was too old and didn't have a chance to win at age forty-six. Nicklaus used the article as motivational fodder and fired a final-round 65 to win the Masters for a record sixth time.

Who has ever told that you can't do something? You might have reacted angrily, with an "I'll show them" attitude with added determination. But if your discouragement came at the wrong time from the wrong person, it could have had a tremendous negative impact on you and deterred you from being all that you could be.

On the other hand, who have we ever written off as not being able to do something? With respect to a person becoming a Christian, have you ever told someone verbally or with body language or with a lack of prayer that there is no way they can come to Christ? We must remember what sinners we were when Jesus cleansed us in the blood of the Lamb for the first time and that there were people who might have prayed for many years for us to come to Christ. "No matter the circumstance, there is no one on God's unreachable list," I once heard Mark Hall of Casting Crowns say. So we must keep praying for those who are, as far as we can tell, not walking with the Lord yet. Everybody has a chance to come to Christ because God is constantly reaching out to them by placing people in their paths. You could be one of those people.

Prayer: Father God, may I not be quick to pass judgment on someone by remembering that at one time, I was a miserable sinner condemned by my past. But through your free gift of grace and my intercessory prayer, each of my friends and family members can come to know Christ. May I do my part in sharing the good news. In Jesus's name, amen.

GOLF 49

$#@%! (How Jesus Cured My Cursing)

Thou shalt not take the Lord's name in vain.

—Exodus 20:7 (KJV)

When I was a teenager, I had a red-hot temper that was fueled by not having Jesus Christ in my life. I was a club-throwing, foul-mouthed, angry young man, and these bad habits carried into my young adult years. When things didn't go my way, I would just go ballistic. I shot 67 one day and broke two clubs. It's not a course record that I'm at all proud of.

Many times, I blamed God for my bad shots, yet he never swung a club. I tell the story that my wife, Becca, gave me a Bible for our third anniversary, perhaps because of a tantrum that I threw on the golf course one day.

Another factor was that it was commonplace and funny to curse on the playing fields or in the dugouts. It was fun to crack jokes, and it seemed harmless at the time, but I later realized how offensive it was to God. I cursed every day for years, either inwardly or outwardly. It seemed to be an incurable habit.

But an amazing thing happened with my temper and with my foul mouth in the first two weeks after I was saved. The Holy Spirit had come into me, but I still needed some time to kick my bad habit. When a car would pull in front of me or I would be surprised, I would let a curse word go before I realized what I had done. But the reactions became fewer and farther between until several weeks later, I was no longer bound by my anger and cursing. I had given up thirty-five years of cursing just as the Jews had given up traditional sacrifices after receiving the Holy Spirit. It was an amazing and almost immediate transformation. Whenever I have doubts or need reassurance, all I need to do is to look back at my transformation, and I know beyond a shadow of a doubt that I have been redeemed.

Tiger Woods took steps to control his behavior on the golf course by going back to Buddhist self-control techniques, but it became quite evident during the final round of the 2010 Masters that he still has a long way to go. A person might try any number of self-improvement techniques, but I speak from truth in my life. The only surefire way to eliminate your unrighteous anger and cursing is to make Jesus Christ the focal point of your life. The power of the Holy Spirit will help you with your daily problems, and one of those problems is certainly cursing, a violation of one of the Ten Commandments. Only Jesus Christ can truly change your life.

Prayer: Father God, I thank you each and every day for the fruit of the Spirit that enables me to keep a lid on it when someone does an injustice to me or I stub my toe or I hit a bad shot. Thank you for your mercy, which I do not deserve, and for forgiving me for all the times I took your name in vain and cursed. In Jesus's name, amen.

GOLF 50

You Really Don't Want to Miss It Here!

Every part of Scripture is God-breathed and useful
one way or another—showing us truth, exposing
our mistakes, correcting our rebellion, training us
to live God's way.

—2 Timothy 3:16 (MSG)

In the 1960s, a man began measuring the golf courses that
the pros play a week in advance. He would draw intricate
diagrams of each hole with many different yardages that
he personally measured. The pros and caddies paid twenty
dollars for each of his special yardage books because they
were extremely valuable and saved them hours of work at
each tour stop. If he sold 150 books at twenty dollars each
for forty courses a year, he made some pretty good money.

The most unique features of the book were the special
notations for the different places on each hole that a player
needed to stay away from, such as deep pot bunkers, water
hazards, or impossible places to pitch close from around
the green. He had a rather unique acronym that I don't
care to repeat here, but in essence, the acronym meant, "You
don't want to end up here!" and "You really don't want to
end up here!" What do the pros call it when they miss it

in these places? They call it dead; meaning, they have no chance to par the hole.

The Bible has great advice for living, including rules to live by such as the Ten Commandments. The Bible also makes it clear that there is pleasure in sin for a season, but the bitterness far outweighs the pleasure. Jesus spent more time talking about the place you don't want to wind up rather than heaven. He used many analogies that the people of the day could relate to, such as wheat and weeds called tares, bridesmaids with no oil in their lamps, and the sheep and the goats. Some will heed the warnings, turn from sin, and turn to Christ. But very sadly, many will not turn.

Have you heeded the warnings? God and Jesus desperately want you to end up with them in heaven, so much so that God is constantly trying to bring you to a relationship with Jesus Christ. Please realize and internalize that the Bible is indeed God-breathed truth.

🚩

Prayer: Most holy and precious God, may I realize that there are some places that I shouldn't be. Give me discernment to stay out of those places, and help me ensure that I will permanently stay out of the ultimate place you really, really don't want us to go for eternity. In Jesus's precious name, amen.

GOLF 51

Bailout!

Matthew 5:27–32, James 4:7, 1 Corinthians 6:18–20

Run from sexual sin!

—1 Corinthians 6:18 (TLB)

A great golf architect builds courses that test the skills of the best players in the world, and he will also make the course playable for the novice golfer from shorter tees. On each hole, the seventeenth at TPC Sawgrass notwithstanding, the architect will design the hole so that there is danger lurking on one side of the fairway such as deep bunkers, out-of-bounds, or water hazards that threaten to swallow your golf ball. On the other side, the architect will leave a safe landing area that is farther from the green. When the golfer plays to the safe area, the second shot will be much more difficult to land on the green for a potential birdie putt.

Oftentimes, the pin placement will be directly over a bunker or near the water hazard. The golfer risks bogey or worse by going directly for the pin to get a birdie, but there is usually a wide area of the green that is accessible. However, the golfer is much more likely to three-putt for bogey after playing safe to the wide area because the putt will be a long one.

The safe areas are called bailouts because the golfer can avoid a serious mistake by bailing out to the safer landing area. Do you realize that God equips us with bailout areas when Satan tempts us with lust? God will never allow us to be tempted beyond our capability to escape. First, God gave us brains to realize that the lure of someone who is not our spouse can be avoided by using the door that God placed in the room. Perhaps one reason God allowed us to invent doors was to give us a way out. Second, he gave us hands to flip magazine covers and to change the TV channel. Third, he gave us necks so that we can turn our heads and avoid taking second looks. Fourth, he gave us legs so that we can run from the temptation of sexual sin. Finally, he gave us Scripture that we can memorize and use against Satan.

It can't happen to you? Yeah, right. No man or woman is immune from succumbing to temptation. Remember that Jesus taught his disciples in the Sermon on the Mount that even thinking about sex outside of marriage is the same as committing the act. But with God's help and the leading of the Holy Spirit, you can find the bailout areas.

Prayer: Father God, help me realize through the Holy Spirit when I am too close to the precipice. I thank you for giving me ears, eyes, hands, and legs that keep me from crossing the edge. In Jesus's name, amen.

GOLF 52

Career Decision

Proverbs 3:5–6

Trust the Lord with all your heart, and do not rely
on your own understanding.

—Proverbs 3:5

Englishman and journeyman golf pro Brian Davis was in
a great position to win his first PGA Tour title as he teed
off on Harbour Town's tough eighteenth hole in a playoff
with veteran Jim Furyk. Davis pulled his second shot into
the hazard to the left of the eighteenth green and faced a
difficult recovery shot. Being careful not to ground his club,
which would have resulted in a two-shot penalty, Davis
carefully swung and played a shot onto the green. As soon
as the ball finished rolling, Davis called over PGA Tour
official Slugger White.

Even the TV announcers were not sure what had hap-
pened. But as Davis took his backswing, he barely nicked
a weed in the hazard. The nick was imperceptible on TV,
but Davis told White that he felt the shaft brush the weed.
Davis incurred a penalty because the club cannot touch
anything in a hazard during the backswing.

What a display of integrity! As Davis rode to the eighteenth tee for the playoff, he must have been thinking that if he won the playoff, he would be in the Masters for the first time. Calling the two-shot penalty on himself immediately assured Davis that he would miss the Masters. Also, his second-place prize money was $400,000 less than Furyk's winning check. But when the pressure was on, he did the right thing immediately. What an absolutely commendable and honorable decision!

When pressure builds for a golfer, the player will often revert to his or her worst habit under pressure. For Tiger and Phil, it's getting stuck on the downswing and slicing the ball. For Kenny Perry, it's the yips with the chips that cost him the 2009 Masters. For Scott Hoch, it was a missed two-footer than cost him the Masters in 1990. There are times when we are all placed in pressure situations.

Who's your daddy when that happens? If your daddy is Satan when the pressure is off, it's likely going to be Satan when the pressure-filled moment comes. Around the house, it could be yelling at your family members. On the road, it could be yelling at the driver who cut you off. On the job or at school, it could be telling a half-truth to protect yourself. But walk in God's presence daily, and you'll make more Christlike decisions when the pressure is on.

Prayer: Father God, help me rely on your strength and the guidance of the Holy Spirit when I must make decisions that could conflict with what I know is the right thing to do. In Jesus's name, amen.

GOLF 53

Cutting Phil by One Shot

Isaiah 40:22, 25–26; John 3:30

It is He that sits upon the circle of the earth, and
the inhabitants thereof are as grasshoppers.

—Isaiah 40:22

Suppose you had an opportunity to play the Pebble Beach Golf Links when it was in US Open condition. The course runs firm and fast, and some of the hole locations are almost impossible to access. *Golf Digest* holds a contest annually when several celebrities and a random golfer are drawn from thousands of entries to see if they can break a hundred. A 10-handicapper would probably break ninety on Pebble Beach during normal conditions, but in Open conditions, the golfer would be hard pressed to break a hundred.

Now suppose the 10-handicapper was paired with Phil Mickelson in the white-hot cauldron of Open pressure. Phil will most likely post a score that is two strokes on either side of par. But 10-handicapper Joe Golfer would do well to break a hundred. Joe Golfer would immediately recognize the difference in their abilities to play tournament golf and know that he's fortunate to be on the same course with Phil. If you took the best score by Phil or Joe on each of the eighteen holes, Joe would likely play just one hole where his score was one stroke better than Phil's. If Phil shot seventy-one, their best ball would be seventy.

It's that same way with God when we think we're doing it all or it's all about us in bringing people to Christ. God chose completely fallible human beings to spread his gospel, but it doesn't happen because of our grandiose plans and positioning. The Holy Spirit is used by God to bring new Christians into the kingdom, yet he chooses to use us as bit players and let us help him out with a shot here or there. Louis Giglio reminded us in his book *I Am Not but I Know I AM* that God is *very, very big* and that we are very, very small. Certainly it is a tremendous honor and privilege whenever someone comes to Christ through an effort we were involved in. But it's the power of God, the saving blood of Jesus Christ, and the drawing of the Holy Spirit that gets the job done. It is the power of God working in us and through us.

Prayer: Father God, help me recognize that it's not the oratory skills that help a person receive Christ, but it is through the power of the Holy Spirit that you use our feeble attempts to bring people to Jesus Christ. Thank you that you allow me to play a small role in the growth of your kingdom, which you and you alone create. In Jesus's name, amen.

GOLF 54

I Don't Look as Good as I Think I Do

Romans 7:18–19

For the good that I would do I do not; but the evil
which I would not, I do.

—Romans 7:19 (KJV)

Allison and Jillian took golf lessons from a golf pro who
used video to show them the proper angles for proper ball
position, backswings, and downswings. The video replays
were very helpful for them to see exactly what their faults
were so that they could correct them.

I once played to a 3-handicap and broke par several
times a year. I had not had my swing videotaped for years
until Chris offered to put my swing on video. I hit eight to
ten iron shots and hit the last few flush. Feeling very confi-
dent, I waited for the video to rewind so I could admire my
swing on the videotape.

What I saw shocked me. As I took the club back, my
head dipped about three inches as I lurched away from the
ball. When my backswing completed, my club was well
past parallel, and the clubface pointed to the right instead
of slightly left of the target. In fact, the club pointed a good

thirty degrees too far to the right. Then I made a nice correction to get the club on line and managed to hit a flush shot, except for the last shot, when I came completely out of the shot and the ball went right. I walked away feeling much more humbled about my golf swing.

We can groove a bad swing and get by most of the time. But in pressure situations, our worst habit will pop up at just the wrong time, and we're in deep trouble. In pressure situations, we can lose our temper or make selfish outbursts, and we wish that we hadn't said it, but it's too late. The damage has been done.

Sometimes we think we're looking good, but we don't realize how sinful our lives are. We have lowered our standards and look all right compared to our peers, but we do not hold our lives up to the standards exemplified by Christ. When we really look at ourselves, and especially our thought lives, we can be confident that we aren't measuring up. That's when it is time to make a confession of our specific flaws and ask God to remove those flaws.

Prayer: Father God, just when I think I am sitting pretty, I can know for sure that I have exalted myself in a prideful manner. Please allow me to make those swing corrections before I have to undertake one of your painful overhauls. In Jesus's name, amen.

GOLF 55

The Spirituality of St. Andrews

Matthew 13:36–50

The tares are gathered and burned in the fire.

—Matthew 13:40

The 150th anniversary edition of the Open Championship was played at the hallowed Old Course at historic St. Andrews, the birthplace of golf. Phil Mickelson said that the course had a spiritual feel to it. Bobby Jones was given the key to the city in 1958. His love affair with St. Andrews was such that he remarked that he would have had a rich and full life even if all he had were his experiences at St. Andrews.

The course has a number of quirks. The players play a blind shot over a railroad shed to the fairway on number seventeen. The fifth hole sports a green that is 101 yards deep, longer than a football field. Imagine putting the length of a football field. The seventh and eleventh holes actually cross as the course loops back toward the club-house. The numbers on the flagsticks on the double greens always add up to eighteen. The course is laced with pot bunkers that are like a one-shot penalty since players must play sideways or even backward because of the steep faces. A fellow with a long-toothed rake walks with the players during the round to rake the bunkers for them.

The spiritual feel that is inescapable comes from a little different twist than the ethereal beauty of Augusta National, which has Amen Corner. Here, the experiences of the players, which often occur in driving rain or howling winds, are described by names that have been given to landmarks on the course. The first hole has a fairway 130 yards wide, and the green sits on the precipice of a creek called the Swilcan Burn. The fourteenth hole par 5 has a ghastly looking bunker shaped like a boomerang that is aptly named Hell Bunker. Jack Nicklaus once took five shots to escape on his way to a 9. The seventeenth hole has a pot bunker that is called the Road Hole Bunker. Tommy Nakajima once made a 13 on this hole, finally escaping what are now called the Sands of Nakajima. The final hole, the eighteenth, is a short par 4 with the most famous bridge in golf, the Swilcan Bridge, and a devilish crevice in front of the green called the Valley of Sin.

Certainly it behooves each of us to escape the Hell Bunkers and the Valleys of Sin and the eternal burn by turning from our sins, trusting in Jesus Christ as Savior and Lord, and staying obedient to God. Jesus Christ is the bridge over the eternal burn. Some competing players have avoided the burn and will escape before their lives are up here on earth. Sadly, some will fall victim to the wages of sin and never escape. In which group do you reside?

Prayer: Father God, thank you for the spiritual context in which these St. Andrews landmarks were named. May these hazards serve as reminders to golfers of the eternal pitfalls that can envelop them without a relationship with Jesus Christ. In Jesus's name, amen.

GOLF 56

When Out of Bounds Is Totally In

But the fruit of the Spirit is love, joy, peace,
patience, goodness, kindness, faithfulness,
gentleness, and self-control.

—Galatians 5:22–23

Here is a story of incredible sportsmanship and grace. Two collegiate golfers, Grant Whybark and Seth Doran, were vying for a spot in the 2010 NAIA National Championship.

Grant's team had wrapped up the conference championship and a trip to nationals, but he found himself in a playoff against Seth for individual honors. The winner would advance to the national tournament. Grant realized that if he won, his opponent and friend, Seth, would not advance. So Grant made a huge decision before he got to the tee box.

Whybark purposely hit his first tee shot out of bounds to the right of the fairway. Amazing! Seth made par and advanced to the national tournament. Grant explained that he did it because Seth is a great player and a great person. Seth had never been to nationals, and this season was his last as a senior. Grant felt like Seth deserved to go to nationals and that he couldn't feel good about taking the chance from him.

What lesson can be learned from Grant? Clearly, he cared more about how his competitor would feel getting to go to nationals than how he would feel if he won the tournament. It was a very selfless act.

This was a great example of grace because Seth received a gift so wonderful that, no matter what a good guy he is, he didn't deserve it. In essence, Grant took one for Seth when he hit his ball out of bounds so that Seth could advance.

Jesus did a similar but much bigger thing for all of us on the cross. He took one for us and paid the penalty so that we could advance to the ultimate tournament: our home in heaven.

Prayer: Father God, in this world of dog-eat-dog competition and win at all costs, thank you for this story that warms our hearts. May I exhibit a similar form of grace to the people that I meet. In Jesus's name, amen.

GOLF 57

Competing for a Greater Cause

Hebrews 11:1–6

What is faith? It is the confident assurance that
something you want is going to happen.

—Hebrews 11:1 (TLB)

On the eve of the Sunday singles final at Medinah Country
Club in the 2012 Ryder Cup, the Europeans trailed 10–6
and had been roundly outplayed by the American team,
having been down 10–4 until winning the last two matches
late Saturday afternoon. But the Europeans still believed
that they could win and were clearly inspired by the late
Seve Ballesteros, who was most instrumental in making
the Ryder Cup a real competition. The European team was
competing for a greater cause.

Although only one team, the 1999 USA team, had
ever erased a four-point margin on Sunday, the Europeans
believed they could come out on top. The odds were even
greater than in 1999 because the Americans were on home
soil and the great majority of fans in the massive gallery
were cheering for them. Also, the American team tradi-
tionally finishes strong in the singles matches. However,

in 2012, the Sunday outcome was the complete opposite because the Americans only garnered three and a half points out of twelve, just as the Europeans only won three and a half points in 1999.

Just as American Captain Crenshaw had done in 1999, the 2012 European Captain Jose Maria-Olazabal front-loaded his lineup and put his top golfers out first in the singles matches. The Europeans won the first four matches to pull even and dominated play on the seventeenth and eighteenth holes, turning two potential losses into wins. Their fans cheered and cheered and sang the European chant over and over, "Ole, ole ole! Ole, ole, ole!"

How did the Europeans pull off the biggest comeback in the history of the Ryder Cup? In 1987, Europe won the Ryder Cup for the first time in America at Muirfield Village in Ohio. The European heroes? Jose Maria-Olazabal and Seve Ballesteros, who formed perhaps the greatest two-man team in the history of the Ryder Cup.

Seve passed away in May 2011, and the captaincy became even more important to Jose-Maria. Olazabal said with tears streaming down his face, "I'm sure Seve is happy where he is today." The Euros thought so much of Seve that they placed Seve's logo—putter raised after his winning putt at the 1988 British Open—on their Ryder Cup bags.

As the Americans faltered on the back nine, the Europeans made big putt after big putt, culminating with Martin Kaymer's gutsy six-footer to win the 2012 Ryder

Cup. Ironically, another German, Bernhard Langer, missed a six-footer at the War on the Shore in 1991 that allowed the Americans to capture the cup. Ironically, Kaymer was viewed as the weakest link on this European team because he had not been in good form after winning the 2010 PGA Championship. Kaymer was mentored by Langer before the matches, and he confided that Bernhard helped him lift his game.

As Christians in Christ's church, we can do great things and overcome tremendous odds if we are united for a greater cause—Jesus Christ. Bonding together under the common purpose of extolling all that Christ was, is, and will be allows us to do uncommon things for the kingdom of God, but only with his help. As Christians, we can learn from this European team, which battled overwhelming odds to claim victory.

Prayer: Most wonderful Father God, thank you for the memory of Seve Ballesteros, who inspired a generation of golfers around the world including twelve men and their captain. May we learn from how they believed in themselves and a greater cause to get the job done at Medinah. May we get the job done for you in our ministries and local churches. In Jesus's name, amen.

GOLF 58

Shooting Past My Headlights

Psalm 119:105, Matthew 6:33, Romans 8:28

Thy word is a lamp unto my feet, and a light unto
my path.

—Psalm 119:105 (KJV)

My mentor, Jim, delighted in the saying, "I'm shooting past my headlights." What he meant was that he was guessing beyond what he could actually see or without having all of the facts. He was shooting in the dark beyond what he really understood.

It was the eve of the 112th US Open Championship in 2012 at the Olympic Club in San Francisco. Olympic is a picturesque, cypress-lined course that is often shrouded in thick fog off the Pacific. The excitement had grown that week because the top golfers included a rejuvenated Tiger Woods and the runaway 2011 US Open champion, Rory McIlroy, who was struggling to recapture his form. Tiger, Phil Mickelson, and Bubba Watson—the popular 2012 Masters champion—were the featured threesome that attracted thousands of followers on Thursday and Friday. The heavyweight pairing reminded longtime golf fans of

Jack Nicklaus, Gary Player, and Arnold Palmer when they were known in the 1960s as the Big Three.

Speaking of Palmer, in 1966 Arnold was thrashing the US Open field at Olympic by seven shots as he walked to the tenth tee on Sunday afternoon. But Arnie was thinking about more than his tee shot on ten. Palmer envisioned the clubhouse celebration where he would receive his second US Open trophy to the delight of his adoring army of fans. Arnie actually set his sights on breaking the US Open scoring record instead of taking care of business on each hole of the back nine. Clearly, he was shooting past his headlights.

Palmer made a couple of bogeys, and Casper made a couple of birdies. Arnie's seemingly insurmountable lead of seven was down to three. Arnie left a six-footer hanging on the front lip on sixteen for another bogey, and he and Casper were now tied. Arnie blew up on the back nine with a forty. Casper fired an outstanding thirty-three and forced an eighteen-hole Monday playoff. In the playoff, Arnie again went out in front, but Casper rallied to beat him. Casper once remarked how tough it was to watch the Sunday back nine collapse by his good friend. The game's most beloved figure not only failed to win his second US Open title, but he never won another major championship. That tournament arguably triggered the decline of Arnie's career on the PGA Tour.

Have you ever been guilty of shooting past your headlights? How about when you are trying to work ahead of

God? Psalm 119:105 reveals that God shines his light in a way that shows us as much as we are ready to see. It's like a farmer with a lantern going to the barn before dawn. He only needs to see one step at a time on the well-worn path to arrive safely. It's easy to be anxious to see the end result and not take care of the business of getting to the finish line. Romans 8:28 (TLB) teaches that "all things are working for our good when we love God and are fitting into his plans." When I do my thing and stop fitting into God's plan, my plan is pretty much toast. God doesn't need me to grow his kingdom, but he would love to use me if I will just work where he is working.

A golfer once led the final round of a major for the first time and found a note in his locker on Sunday. The note was from a fellow pro, and it read, "Fairways and greens, cuz." His friend's advice was to play one shot at a time. Hit the fairway, then hit the green. Don't get ahead of yourself out there. That's good advice for life. Take it one day at a time with God, and trust God with the end result. Let's focus on him daily with an active prayer life and frequent reading and study of the Bible, and seek his kingdom first (Matthew 6:33).

⛳

Prayer: Most merciful and gracious God, if I could just learn to be patient and not run ahead of you, I know that

I could help you more. Remind me when I shoot past my headlights and try to do it on my own without you. In the precious name of our Lord and Savior Jesus Christ, amen.

GOLF 59

Webb's Prayer

Luke 18:1, Philippians 4:6, Romans 12:12
1 Thessalonians 5:17

Be patient in trouble and prayerful always.

—Romans 12:12 (TLB)

Webb Simpson won the 2012 US Open at the Olympic Club in San Francisco. Simpson shot 68–68 on the weekend and waited in the clubhouse with his wife, Dowd, as veteran Jim Furyk bogeyed sixteen and eighteen to lose by one shot. The win was especially sweet for Webb, a former recipient of the Arnold Palmer scholarship at Wake Forest University, because Olympic was the site of Arnold Palmer's most heartbreaking loss in the 1966 US Open. Billy Casper, who was the golfer that beat Palmer in the 1966 playoff, was present for the awards ceremony on the eighteenth green that evening. How is that for irony!

A few fun facts about Webb, who was probably an unknown to all but the most avid golf fans. He won two PGA Tour tournaments in 2011 and led the tour in All-Around statistics, which reflects his consistent play. Webb bears a startling resemblance to a young Matthew Perry, the actor from *Friends*. He is a father of two young children, and his wife, Dowd, was seven months pregnant as she followed him for all seventy-two holes at Olympic. Last but not least, Simpson is a believer, a follower of Jesus Christ. In fact, believers swept the first two majors of 2012, Bubba Watson being the Masters winner.

Webb has been known to tweet Bible verses to his followers on Twitter. Earlier in 2012 at New Orleans, he sported a Titleist cap with Isaiah 63 sewn in the back. At Augusta, he wrote down verses from 1 Corinthians to help him stay focused. He commented after the Sunday US Open round, "I've never prayed as much as I did over the last three holes." Webb prayed that he would remain calm under pressure. The calm that he received from praying helped him handle the pressure down the stretch, particularly when he got up and down from a very difficult lie near the eighteenth green.

What do you think about Webb, praying down the stretch? Did Simpson have an advantage over other players who didn't pray? Did God help him win his first major because he prayed? Let's see what the Bible says about prayer. Luke 18:1 says that "men ought to pray and not to lose heart." It would have been easy to lose heart on that tough course where not one golfer shot even par for seventy-two holes! Philippians 4:6 says, "Do not worry about anything, but in everything by prayer and supplication with thanksgiving, let your requests be made known to God."

Simpson was not praying to win or to not make bogeys, but he prayed to stay calm and receive help in handling the intense pressure. Romans 12:12 (TLB) says, "Be patient in trouble and prayerful always." The US Open is the ultimate test of patience in golf. Certainly, there was plenty of trouble to contend with. Simpson even said he was so amped up that he could not feel his legs at times.

How do you feel about praying before and during a competition? I say go for it because it pleases God when we involve him in all aspects of our lives. If we only go to him after we've just made a mess of things or suffered a defeat, he isn't nearly as pleased. God loves it when we involve him in the little stuff and when things are going well. According to 1 Thessalonians 5:17, we are to "pray without ceasing."

Prayer: Most wonderful Holy Father, it is so great and so reassuring that you are always there for me, regardless of circumstance. Thank you for your mercies that are new every day. In Jesus's name, amen.

GOLF 60

Deep Cuts

And by His wounds, we are healed.

—Isaiah 53:5 (TLB)

In the 1970s, there were many fewer quality golf balls on the market compared to the wide selection in 2013. My favorite golf ball from the seventies was the Titleist Tour Professional with a balata cover. This ball had a soft cover and a liquid-rubber inner core, which was encased by thousands of thin rubber bands. When it rained and you couldn't play golf, it was great fun to peel the cover off and unravel the rubber bands to expose the red rubber core.

The Titleist ball came in two compressions—one hundred and ninety. The one hundred had a black number, which is how you could distinguish it from a ninety, which had a red number. The one hundred went a few yards farther than the ninety, especially in hot weather. This balata-covered ball had a great feel against an iron or persimmon wood, and it made a Top-Flite feel like a rock. The ball had great spin, and you could really draw it back with a wedge, just like the pros.

But the Titleist balata ball had one little drawback. If you strike the ball with the leading edge of a 9-iron or wedge, the blade would pierce the cover. The ball would be smiling at you, but you won't be smiling back. The cover would be sliced open in the shape of a crescent moon, and the ball would no longer be round. You would be forced to take it out of play because you couldn't putt true with it. No matter how hard you press on the dented cover with your thumb, you could not remove that smile. It will hurt your wallet because the Titleist balata is also the most expensive ball. Those Titleists with the deep cuts ended up in your range bag, never to be used again in a round of golf.

There is a big range bag of lives with deep emotional, physical, and spiritual cuts that need healing. Perhaps you made a grievous mistake or someone wronged you in a way that left you with a scar like those Titleists. Perhaps you were judged or shunned by people in a church, and you decided that you would never set foot in any church again. You may believe that your scar is with you for the rest of your life no matter what happens. Perhaps you feel abandoned by society or you have chosen to withdraw, or you know someone who has withdrawn or feels rejected.

But there is always hope because there is one who can heal your hurts, and his name is Jesus. The prophet Isaiah foretold that Jesus would be despised and rejected by men (53:3) and would be led as a lamb to the slaughter (53:7). Jesus suffered the deepest wounds imaginable when the Roman soldiers laid his back open with their bone-encrusted whips. Jesus was scorned with vicious verbal threats on the way to the cross and on the cross by the angry mob that sought to kill him. Christ, and his Father God who sent him, loved us so much that he took the thirty-nine lashes for all mankind so that someday our deepest cuts could be healed by his life-giving blood. The spilled blood from Jesus's wounds can cover our sadness, our guilt, our helplessness, and our sins if we will only ask God for forgiveness and healing.

Prayer: Most gracious God, I turn to you for healing from any deep cuts that have left me alienated from others and have separated me from you. Thank you for the life-saving blood of your Son, Jesus Christ, which can heal my scars and make me whole again. In the name of Jesus, amen.

Unlocking Perfection

Romans 12:1–2, Philippians 1:6

And do not be conformed to this world, but be transformed by the renewing of your mind, so that you may prove what is that good and acceptable and perfect will of God.

—Romans 12:2

There is an old saying that your best golf shots come on the last couple of holes because after a day of discouragement, the golfing gods allow your best shots to happen then so that you will come back again for more frustration! I experienced that feeling in a scramble tournament after I had struggled with inconsistency all day long. On our seventeenth hole, I hit a drive down the middle, hit the three-quarter wedge shot with the feel that I had been looking for all day, and stuffed the eight-foot putt right in the center. On our eighteenth hole, I stroked a forty-foot putt to the top tier of the green and into the heart of the cup! Where had that been all day?

It was a great way to finish the round, but it started me thinking. The wedge and those two putts were as pure as any tour player could have struck. It's just those tens of mediocre shots that separated me from the best! Every golfer has the capability of playing perfect shots, but they don't materialize because of any combination of physical, mental, and emotional factors. The best golfers find a way to produce those perfect shots much more frequently than average golfers, which is why we are thankful for our day jobs!

As believers, we have perfection inside us in the form of the Holy Spirit as a person. But the gunk and residue that is created by our sinful nature often blocks people from seeing the perfection of the Holy Spirit. We have those perfect moments inside us, but they get out much less often than God would like to see.

What can we do? Keep striving for perfection. Keep trying and realize that we're going to botch some things. Be patient with the ones we love and realize they're going to botch some things too. Sure, we'll never attain perfection in this lifetime, but we can attain more perfect moments that allow his light to shine brilliantly for all to see.

Annika Sorenstam once said that her goal was to shoot a 54, which would be a birdie on every hole! There will come a day when we hit all the fairways and greens and sink all the putts. That day will be the day that Christ makes us complete in him (Philippians 1:6).

Prayer: Father God, I know that I can do much better than I have been demonstrating. Help me to overcome my self-ishness so that people see more of the Holy Spirit and less of me. In Jesus's name, amen.

GOLF 62

Good Morning, Larry!

The Lord knows those that are His.

—2 Timothy 2:19

Larry Mize, the 1987 Masters champion, sponsored a golf tournament for a number of years that raised money benefiting the Cystic Fibrosis Foundation of Atlanta. The Golf Club of Georgia hosted the event, and my friend Tim invited me to play in 1995. What a treat! In addition to playing a prestigious, well-manicured golf course, I received two new Cleveland Classic wedges at the registration table! I was having a blast, and we hadn't even teed off yet!

At the time, I was six feet tall and 160 pounds, and I wore a white visor over my slightly long hair. As I walked to the practice range to hit all the free range balls that I wanted, a man in a golf cart approached me. *Gee, he is really staring at me*, I thought. As I met him, he said in a very reverential tone, "Good morning, Larry!" Ha, he thought that I was Larry Mize! It happened again before I got to the practice tee. "Good morning, Larry!" I was on cloud nine.

There was enough visible evidence to make two people think that I was Larry Mize. There was also enough visible evidence in my life to make people believe that I was a Christian. I coordinated one of the most popular youth basketball leagues in East Cobb at Mt. Zion UMC. But my life did not reflect the Savior when I left the church property, and the Lord knew "that I was not His" (2 Timothy 2:19).

Our pro that day was Hicks Malonson, who was from my club in Marietta. Hicks tried to make the PGA Tour for several years before giving up his dream. Twelve years later in 2007, I spoke to the youth at a Marietta church. The gentleman teaching the eleven o'clock class gave me his business card. It was Hicks! He and I were reunited as brothers in Christ!

Prayer: Most gracious Heavenly Father, how wonderful it is to look back and know that I am saved, just like Larry and Hicks, and can join them for a wonderful reunion on the first tee in heaven one fine day. In your loving name, Jesus. Amen.

GOLF 63

Bubba Golf

1 Thessalonians 5:11, Romans 12:10

Therefore encourage one another and build each
other up.

—1 Thessalonians 5:11 (NIV)

America discovered a new golf hero in 2012. His name is
Bubba Watson, and he hails from the little town of Bagdad,
Florida. Prior to his Masters win, he was best known as a
left-handed, lanky, long-ball hitting, and flamboyant golfer.
After he won the 2012 Masters on Easter Sunday, he tear-
fully thanked his Lord and Savior Jesus Christ at the green
jacket ceremony on the putting green.

The Masters patrons and all of America were cheering
for this new hero. He made just enough putts to win, and
he blasted 350-yard tee shots and carved unbelievable slices
and hooks. Bubba is the American version of the great
Spanish golfer, the late Severiano Ballesteros.

Often thwarted by being too hard on himself, Bubba
kept his composure throughout the back nine and bird-
ied four consecutive holes. On the second playoff hole, he
played *the* most amazing shot after he drove into the trees

to the right of the tenth fairway. Through a small opening, Bubba hooked his fifty-two-degree wedge forty yards to the right and wound up ten feet from the hole. The gallery lining the entire right side of the fairway went crazy. Bubba two-putted for the win and tearfully hugged his mother on the tenth green as they remembered Bubba's father, who passed away in 2011.

What was especially touching to me was how Rickie Fowler, Ben Crane, and Aaron Baddeley congratulated their brother in Christ with hugs on the tenth green! My wife, Becca, asked me if it was unusual for other players to follow their peers during a playoff. I responded that it was much more common for the European players to do so, and I pointed out that those were Bubba's brothers in Christ.

Not only did Bubba win on Easter Sunday, but he won just two weeks after he and his wife Angie adopted a baby boy!

As Christian brothers and sisters, we are supposed to support each other in good times and bad. We read in 1 Thessalonians 5:11 (NIV) that we are "to encourage one another and build each other up." Receiving support from Christian brothers or sisters is one of the tremendous blessings of being a Christian.

Update: Rickie Fowler notched his first PGA Tour victory in Charlotte just four weeks after the Masters by making birdie on the first playoff hole. Surely, the encouragement that Rickie received from his tour brothers in Christ helped him down the stretch.

Prayer: Father God, thank you for every brother or sister in Christ who ever gave me encouragement when I needed it most. May I return the same support to them and always look for ways to build them up as the evil one seeks to tear them down. In the precious name of Jesus Christ, amen.

GOLF 64

Back to the Basics

Our Father, which art in heaven, hallowed be
thy name. Thy kingdom come, thy will be done,
on earth as it is in heaven. Give us this day our
daily bread, and forgive us of our trespasses, as we
forgive those who trespass against us. And lead us
not into temptation, but deliver us from evil. For
thine is the kingdom, the power, and the glory,
forever and ever. Amen.

—Matthew 6:9–13

Jack Nicklaus became the greatest major champion in the
history of golf with eighteen professional victories. He
took lessons from a gentleman named Jack—Jack Grout—
who was the head professional at Scioto Country Club in
Columbus, Ohio. Grout taught Jack throughout middle
school, high school, college, and his pro career.

In high school, Jack played football and basketball, so
he took a break from golf during the winter. When he
came back for golf in the spring, Grout would always take
him back to the basics. This pattern continued long into
Jack's professional career. When Jack would get ready to go

back out on tour, he would go see Grout or fly him down to Florida.

Grout would always make the same first request of Jack each year. He would say, "Let me see your grip." Nicklaus would grip the club and hold his hands for Grout to make sure they fit properly. Why would a major championship winner be asked to do such an elementary thing that he had done since he was a kid? Grout wanted to make sure that Jack started off correctly since the grip is the first fundamental of a sound swing. Even a seasoned veteran could fall into a bad habit of an unsound grip that could take months to correct.

Even mature Christians need to come back to the basics, and one of the most fundamental habits is reciting the Lord's Prayer, both in private and in public whenever possible. Jesus's disciples said, "Lord, teach us to pray." Jesus taught them this simple prayer, which covers all the bases, from following God's will to glorifying God to worshipping his holy name to thanks for daily provisions to forgiveness to being protected from temptation brought on by Satan. No matter how old we are, reciting the Lord's Prayer is a great way to honor God and not just in church on Sunday morning.

Prayer: Dear Jesus, thank you for teaching me this great fundamental prayer that I can fall back on time and time again, knowing that every time I say the prayer earnestly, it pleases and honors you and your Father. In Jesus's name, amen.

GOLF 65

Caught Red-Handed

He is…watching everything that concerns you.

—1 Peter 5:7 (TLB)

The Mark Richt Northeast Georgia Fellowship of Christian Athletes (FCA) Golf Tournament raised money to send high school athletes to summer FCA camp. FCA has a high success rate of reaching kids for Christ during the summer when they are free from distractions to hear the word of God. I was always motivated to take a team over to Athens, believing that out of our collective contributions, the odds were that a kid on our nickel would come into the kingdom.

In 2010, our team had completed play; and as I walked toward the scoreboard, I realized that I had misplaced the scorecard. I searched but could not find the card. Our ten-under par score was not a threat to win, place, or show, so I grabbed a spare card off the nearest cart. Knowing what we had scored on each hole, I began to fill out the card.

At that moment, my good friend Kip and two of his teammates walked by. Kip teased me by saying, "Dan, I know what you're doing. You've already walked up to the scoreboard to see what the best score is, and now you're filling out your card!"

His comments caught me off guard and left me momentarily speechless. I grinned and said, "Kip, you caught me red-handed. What can I say?" It never occurred to me that people have actually done what Kip described in order to win a tournament or a prize. Because he had just finished play, he couldn't have known that I had already walked to the scoreboard. We had a hearty laugh over it.

That embarrassing little episode reminded me that God knows our every move, and our actions need to be predicated on pleasing and honoring him. He knows our ways, our motives, our thoughts, our private actions, and our public actions. We need to always honor him in every situation. Because God knows everything about us, even when we don't think that God is watching.

Prayer: Father God, thank you for friends that tease me in a loving way. Even when it stings a little, may I maintain my sense of humor and return the favor in a nonthreatening manner. Thank you for watching me and watching over me. In Jesus's name, amen.

GOLF 66

Cleaning the Line

If we confess our sins, He is faithful and just and
will forgive us our sins, and cleanse us from all
unrighteousness.

—1 John 1:9

One way to spot a lower handicap golfer putting for a
birdie or a novice player putting for a par is to watch how
diligently the player clears the line for the putt. The low
handicapper might just go ahead and putt for a par with
tiny debris in his line. However, if he has a good chance for
a birdie, he will make sure that his line to the hole is clear of
any and all debris—large or microscopic. The obstacles that
he removes include loose sand that was splashed from bun-
kers, unrepaired ball marks, dry leaves, and the prickly sta-
men that flew into Phil Mickelson's line on the second hole
of the final round of the 2009 Masters. The golfer carefully
removes all impurities from his line so that he can roll the
ball over the perfectly manicured green and into the hole.

To remain in right standing with God, we need to make
sure all impurities (sins) are confessed and removed from
our hearts. To become pure again, it is necessary to confess

all the specific sins that separate us from God. As meticulously as the golfer cleans the line for the birdie putt, we need to be meticulous about confessing our sins to our Father in heaven and asking for forgiveness. God will always forgive each sin that is presented to him in godly sorrow and give us a clear conscience that is free from debris.

Prayer: Father God, help me become more diligent in identifying and presenting specific sins that are hindering my relationship with you. May I readily confess them to you and enjoy a renewed cleansing made possible by the precious blood of my Savior and Lord, Jesus Christ. In Jesus's name, amen.

GOLF 67

Unleash His Power

You are endued with power from on high.

—Luke 24:49

On Sunday at the 1986 Masters, Jack Nicklaus was three shots back as he stood on the fifteenth tee. He unleashed a powerful drive, which left him with only a 4-iron to the green. After a shot to fifteen feet, Jack made the eagle putt, birdied the next two holes, and went on to win the Masters for his sixth green jacket! Jack drove the golf ball twenty yards farther than normal by unleashing extra power and clubhead speed to get into a position to reach the green. He needed the extra distance desperately in order to trigger his comeback. By reaching the green with a midiron, he hit the ball high enough with enough spin to land it softly near the cup.

The Holy Spirit gives us reserve power when we need something extra. When a special challenge or problem occurs in our lives, we can look inwardly to the Holy Spirit, who is God in us, and ask for special help and strength to meet the challenge. What a blessed feeling to know that we've got extra power from God at our disposal on the days that we need it most!

Prayer: Father God, thank you for the supernatural power, which you give us through the Holy Spirit within us. Help me remember to tap into your power whenever I need it. In the name of Jesus, amen.

GOLF 68

Q-School Pressure

I can do all things through Christ
who strengthens me.

—Philippians 4:13

There is nothing more pressure-packed than the final day of the PGA Tour Web.com Qualifying School, or Q-School. Thousands of players in three stages of qualifying have been whittled down to approximately one hundred players vying for twenty-five spots. The third and final stage of Q-School is an exhausting six consecutive rounds. Even PGA tournaments are only four rounds. A pro will miss qualifying by one shot, and he will be forced to wait an entire year before attempting to get on the tour. That yearlong wait is why the pressure is so excruciating.

Joe Daley faced a six-foot putt on the eighteenth hole of the final round of Q-School. If he made the putt, he would qualify to play on the PGA Tour. The ball rolled toward the center of the cup, struck the plastic rim, which had not been tamped down sufficiently, and bounced back, coming to rest on the front lip of the cup.

Previous failures can play in the heads of the golfers, making it more difficult to play well, and the pressure builds, sending the golfer into a downward spiral. Mac O'Grady participated in seventeen Q-Schools before finally earning his PGA Tour card.

Failure in our lives can have a similar effect. Satan constantly tells our subconscious, "You can't do it. You'll never amount to anything. Look, you messed up again. Just give up." That's when we need to listen to the Truth, Jesus Christ, who tells us through the Holy Spirit that we can face the seemingly impossible and that we can get it done despite all odds. Through Christ who strengthens us, anything is possible and we can succeed. When we give it our very best, even if we fall short of our desired outcome, we can still be successful in God's eyes.

Doomed by past failures or simply the fear of failure? To never fail means to never go for it. Jesus assures us that we can do it, whether it's Peter walking on water or it's us facing a difficult task. We can do it with the help of Jesus, the One who gives us strength.

Prayer: Most wonderful Father, I am so grateful for the encouragement and hope that lives within me because of the strength that you give me through your Son, Jesus Christ. In Jesus's name I pray, amen.

GOLF 69

Reading the Green

All Scripture is given by inspiration of God…
that the man of God may be complete, thoroughly
equipped for every good work.

—2 Timothy 3:16–17

Watching the Masters gives golf fans a chance each year to see some of the most astonishing twists and turns on any greens in golf, especially the diabolical fourteenth green, whose huge mounds make it look like an elephant is buried in the middle of the green. On the fourteenth and sixteenth greens, it's commonplace to see putts break fifteen to twenty feet from certain positions on the green. It takes incredible skill to get the first putt close to the hole.

Reading the green in golf means determining how much putts are going to break. There are many different techniques. Some golfers crouch behind the ball. Others hold the putter shaft perpendicular to the slope of the green. By lining up the shaft just to the left edge of the ball, you see exactly where to aim the putt. Camilo Villegas uses the spider technique by putting his entire body parallel to the ground to look directly down the line at ground level.

Other factors must be considered, especially on Bermuda greens, such as the amount of grain, the slope of the green, and the speed of the green. When putts are down grain, they are much faster. When putting into the grain, the putts are much slower. The slope of the green must be taken into account when putting downhill and uphill. All of these intricacies must be analyzed to get the correct read. If the golfer doesn't make the correct read, putting is merely guesswork, and the chance of holing a putt is slim. If the read is correct, then you need a perfect stroke and perfect speed to hole the putt. Most professional golfers will ask their caddies for assistance in reading greens. Their advice helps them make the best possible decisions.

Just as reading the green is crucial to the success of the golfer, reading the Bible is crucial for every believer. If a believer goes through life reading the Bible, studying passages, memorizing verses, phrases, and even individual words, God will reveal the "true break" of the passages so that you can apply them confidently in your daily walk. When you aren't sure what a passage means, ask a pastor, a Christian brother or sister, a small group, or Bible Study group to help you get the "correct read" to apply the truth effectively in your life. You can also access online Bible commentaries, which explain chapters verse by verse, and read different translations such as the New International Version (NIV), English Standard Version (ESV), The Message (MSG), and The Voice.

God gave his people the Living Word so that we can get the best possible read on our lives that can be fraught with deceptive twists, turns, and slippery slopes.

Prayer: Father God, thank you for equipping us with your word. When situations are hard to read like tricky greens, we can turn to the Bible for guidance on what we should do. Thank you for your eternal word. In the precious name of our Savior and Lord, Jesus Christ, amen.

GOLF 70

The Marker

Acts 20:24, Romans 8:28

But my life is worth nothing unless I use it for doing the work assigned me by the Lord Jesus.

—Acts 20:24

Every Masters participant is hopeful of winning when he enters the fabled grounds on Monday morning. The first three days of practice are full of anticipation as the players hone their games before the first big tee shot on Thursday. Reality quickly sets in when the golfer makes his first bogey or two. When a golfer is three or four over par, the elation goes from visions of the green jacket to surviving to play on the weekend.

On Friday afternoon, there is one person who has a perspective different from any player in the field. That person is the marker. A marker is a noncompeting golfer who plays with a Masters participant on Saturday and Sunday if the number of players who make the cut is an odd number. The marker is hoping for an odd number! The marker helps the participant, who otherwise would have played alone, maintain a normal pace of play.

For instance, in the 2011 Masters, fifty-one players made the cut. A marker went out with Ernie Els early Saturday morning. Undoubtedly, the marker was thrilled to play and had probably practiced for weeks with the hope that he would play. The marker probably felt a sense of elation getting to tee off on a beautiful Saturday morning and Sunday morning. Many patrons may not have realized the marker was not a participant. He enjoyed the applause of the patrons for his birdies and pars. He didn't even play out the hole if he messed up, because he didn't want to slow down the player whose score in the tournament counts. The marker has no risk. He enjoys the play, but in the end, he's not really in the game.

Bobby Clampett was a rising young star in golf. Early in his career, he played in the 1979 US Open but missed the cut after the first two days. On Saturday morning, he went out to play as a marker with another competitor. He entertained the fans by hitting a couple of tee shots off his knees. The fans loved it! However, the news filtered back to USGA chairman P. J. Boatwright, who yanked Bobby off the course.

A good marker does not call attention to himself. He quietly goes about his business and allows his playing partner to have the best conditions under which to play. The marker allows his playing partner to receive the glory and always puts the other player ahead of himself.

Christians need to prepare like the marker. Be where we are supposed to be and do what we are supposed to do by following God's plan for our lives (see Romans 8:28). Practice daily with the hope that there will be an opportunity to play in the field for God. Stay ready to perform. Enjoy and appreciate the opportunity. Follow God's lead and don't draw attention to ourselves because it's not about us. Put others first, and give God the glory.

I wouldn't call Jesus a marker, but his work for his Father had some parallels. He was all about doing his Father's work and doing it in a humble way that would not draw undue attention to himself. Often he performed miracles for people and told them not to say anything. He followed his Father's pace of play and his plan. Jesus allowed his Father to receive the glory, and he was present solely to fulfill the mission for which his Father sent him.

Prayer: Lord Jesus, may I be true to you and perform my deeds in a way that draws attention to you, my Savior and Lord, and gives our Father the glory. In Jesus's name, amen.

GOLF 71

A Golfer's Greatest Ally

Proverbs 3:6, Romans 8:26

The Holy Spirit helps us with our daily problems.

—Romans 8:26 (TLB)

Every champion golfer has benefited from a reliable caddie, who performs a number of important functions. The caddie obviously carries the fifty-pound golf bag around the course so his golfer doesn't get tired. He reads the green when his golfer needs a second opinion on a putt. The caddie offers encouragement and even humor to lighten the mood in a tense situation. He gives advice when his golfer cannot decide which club to use.

A great example of a caddie being really on his game is when he backs his man off a shot when course conditions change. Suppose Phil Mickelson has 178 yards to a flagstick cut very close to the water with a 15 mile-per-hour wind coming across from left to right. Just before Phil begins his backswing, the wind shifts directly into him. Bones Mackay, his caddy, says, "Hold it, Phil!" Now that takes a lot of nerve to back your man off a crucial shot, but it would have been the difference between the ball in the water or the ball on the green. Phil would appreciate the bold gesture because they've developed a close relationship over the years, and he trusts Bones. Phil has learned to listen to Bones. If Bones says back off, Phil backs off. Not all golfers and their caddies develop relationships that are that close and trusting.

It's this kind of close relationship that we need with the Holy Spirit, who is God in us. When we face a significant challenge or important decision, we need to consult God through the Holy Spirit and listen for direction. Before we make the risky move, the Holy Spirit will let us know if our action is not a good idea. If sin is present in our lives, blocking our discernment, we may go ahead and "hit the shot" that ends up working against us. Consulting the Holy Spirit through prayer and being open to his guidance will result in clearer direction for us to follow.

The next time you see a caddie call his pro off a shot, know that there is a good team working there. It's the kind of teaming you and I need with the Holy Spirit to make the best choices with the least negative consequences.

Prayer: Father God, I am so thankful that you sent the Holy Spirit to live inside of me and to give me guidance just before I am about to make a bad choice. Thank you for your eternal presence through the Spirit. In the name of Jesus Christ who came to save us, amen.

GOLF 72

Celebration

Matthew 28:1–6

He is not here, for He is risen as He said. Come,
see the place where the Lord lay.

—Matthew 28:6

Masters Week 2011 was the perfect time for recalling and celebrating one of the greatest Masters finishes ever. It had been twenty-five years since Jack Nicklaus won the 1986 Masters with a scintillating come-from-behind win after a back-nine thirty. Nicklaus was on the ninth green when Tom Kite and Seve Ballesteros pitched in from the fairway for back-to-back eagles on the eighth hole. After the second roar, Jack turned to the gallery where I was standing behind the greenside bunker and said, "Let's make some noise of our own." He promptly drained the fifteen-foot birdie putt to the delight of the crowd and was off to the races!

Jack birdied ten and eleven with long putts, eagled the fifteenth hole, almost made a hole in one on the sixteenth and made the putt that is replayed time and time again every April when the Masters is promoted. Jack had a fifteen-foot slightly downhill putt on seventeen. Jack stroked the putt, and as the ball nears the hole, Verne Lundquist, the CBS announcer in the tower on fifteen, says, "Maybe," then "Yes, sir!" when the ball drops into the cup. The birdie gave Jack the lead that he would never relinquish. Jack snatched victory from the jaws of defeat and became the oldest Masters champion at age forty-six. This twenty-fifth anniversary of Jack's comeback brought renewed attention to the greatest Masters ever in the opinion of many fans and experts.

I was on the back nine at Augusta, watching my golfing idol make history. The roars were so loud after his putts on fifteen and sixteen, the hair literally stood up on the back of my neck. There had been a mixture of groans and cheers when Seve Ballesteros fatted a 4-iron into the water on fifteen. I remember vividly how my friend Cora, Jack's biggest fan at Augusta, screamed when we were standing by the rope to the right of the seventeenth fairway, "Jack, Seve's in the water!"

There is another event that is celebrated each spring that has far more significance than any other event in history. In fact, it's been replayed every spring when the dogwoods bloom for almost two thousand years. The story is Easter, the triumph over tragedy by Jesus Christ, who went to the cross and rose from the grave to defeat death forever, which is known as the Resurrection. Christ snatched victory from the jaws of defeat by beating the grave. Because Jesus was resurrected from the grave, we can put our faith in him, knowing that our sins can be fully buried and forgiven.

Prayer: Dear Father, thank you for the story that we love to retell over and over again. It's the one about the Son of God, who you brought back from the dead so that I could have eternal life. In Jesus's name, amen.

GOLF 73

Let's Give Him the Glory

Psalm 150

Let everything that has breath praise the Lord.
Praise the Lord!

—Psalm 150:6

In 1987, the year after arguably the greatest Masters in golf history, came a three-way playoff between Greg Norman, Seve Ballesteros, and unheralded Augusta native Larry Mize. Greg and Seve were the swashbuckling fan favorites of international fame, and the two of them along with Mize had tied after seventy-two holes to force a playoff on number ten.

Seve bogeyed ten to fall out of the playoff, and I recall seeing him trudge sadly uphill back to the clubhouse through the long shadows of the hundred-foot slope of the tenth fairway. An enormous crowd gathered on eleven at Amen Corner as Mize and Norman played their second shots. Mize pushed his second well right of the green, over one hundred feet from the flagstick. Norman played an iron thirty feet from the cup.

I was having great difficulty seeing the action because there were so many people, but I saw a golf cart parked to the right of the twelfth tee. I grabbed the top of the cart, carefully placed my spiked golf shoes on the back right fender, and swung myself up to be a full two feet above anyone else. I had a perfect view, but I didn't consider the consequences if I had slipped, which could have happened. I might have written golf history, never to live it down.

Mize played a perfect Scottish-type bump and run. The ball took two skips, ran onto the green, and rolled toward the hole. *Man, this looks good!* I thought when the ball was a few feet from the cup. It went in! Larry leaped into the air, thrust his fists skyward, and pumped his arms bent at the elbow. How he kept from screaming himself is beyond me. Several thousand fans at Amen Corner just went berserk for the local kid who grew up in Augusta and no doubt had envisioned a similar shot to win the Masters many times in his boyhood.

That's when he did it. In the midst of the raucous celebration, Larry placed his palms together with his elbows out in the universal symbol of prayer and looked heavenward to give God thanks. Five seconds after the most thrilling shot he had ever made or would ever make, Mize gave thanks to God. Did God make the ball go in because Mize is a believer? I don't think so. But the believer who played the unbelievable shot paused and gave him thanks.

In the midst of all our blessings, small or miraculous, let's pause to give God thanks and give him the glory, the honor, and the praise. What is really cool is how that shot gave a young pro an opportunity to tell that story and share his faith with thousands. God is good all the time. All the time, God is good.

Prayer: Father God, sometimes athletes are judged wrongly when they acknowledge you on the playing field. May you give them the blessings that they deserve for the genuine demonstrations of thankfulness, faith, and gratitude. In the name of Jesus, amen.

GOLF 74

Digging in the Dirt

All Scripture is given by inspiration of God, and is
profitable for doctrine, for reproof, for correction,
for instruction in righteousness, that the man of
God may be complete, thoroughly equipped for
every good work.

—2 Timothy 3:16–17

When Jillian was seven, she and I went to the River Pines driving range. She had a very good swing, and I recall two guys watching her hit the little five-wood that I had cut down for her.

She turned to me and said, "Daddy, I made a diggit."

I said, "You made a what?"

"A diggit." She pointed to the ground.

I said, "Oh, you mean a divot." We laughed because it made perfect sense that you "dig" into the ground when you hit a shot.

Legend has it that Ben Hogan found his golf game in the dirt. During his early professional years, he fought a snap hook that kept him from winning. Hogan pounded balls and pounded balls until he got his swing right. How did he know that his swing was sound or needed work? He looked at the dirt. Hogan studied the pattern of his divots. If his divots were too deep, his swing plane was too steep. If his iron only scraped the top of the ground, his swing plane was too shallow. If his divots pointed to the left, which my divots tend to do, he was cutting across the ball and hitting a slice. Eventually, Hogan got it right and became one of the greatest golfers in history. Sixty years later, he is still the pro that other pros talk about as the man who literally dug his swing out of the dirt.

When I watch the best golfers in the world, I admire the divot patterns that they make over and over again. Their divots are about the width and length of a dollar bill and about one-fourth-inch thick. They look just like beaver tails. A PGA Tour pro will carve out a rectangular box that is perfectly symmetrical as he goes through the irons in his bag. If his swing is a little off, he can spot it and correct it before playing the course and making mistakes. On my best swings, I might come close to their divot patterns, but you can look in the dirt and know that I am really grateful to break eighty.

Want to develop consistency and power in your life? Dig into the Bible, God's book for giving us the answers to our questions. When we find the answers, we live more consistently for the kingdom. Through the Bible, the sword of the Spirit, we find the power to live our lives boldly and passionately. It's not our power, but God's power exhibited through the Holy Spirit within us. If you find yourself drifting off course, the Bible will help you diagnose the problem and correct it before you go out-of-bounds.

Just as you must be willing to put in the hard work of digging in the dirt to build a good golf swing, you've got to be willing to put in the hard work of digging into the Bible to find the truths that will bring you closer to God, closer to living out his plan for your life, and closer to the joy that only he can give you. Find the answers to your golf swing by digging in the dirt. Find the answers to godly living and eternal life by digging into the mighty, unchanging, everlasting word of God.

Prayer: Father God, help me remember each day that the keys to righteous living and peace in my life are only a two-foot putt away when I put down the remote and reach for your Word. In Jesus's Holy name, amen.

GOLF 75

Second Place

Psalm 73, Matthew 13:42, Hebrews 10:30–31

There will be weeping and gnashing of teeth.

—Matthew 13:42

Tiger Woods was a college student and a member of the Stanford University golf team when he fired a final-round sixty-six in the 1996 Open Championship. His score drew the attention of golf fans and was a sign of outstanding play to come over the next dozen years.

After his round, he was interviewed and asked what he thought of his showing. Already the winner of more than one hundred amateur tournaments worldwide, Tiger started his reply with, "Second sucks." Curtis Strange was in the ABC booth, and after he heard Tiger's brash statement, he chuckled, "Oh, he'll learn. Just wait until he gets out on tour. He'll change his mind."

But Tiger was out there to win, winning his third US Amateur at Pumpkin Ridge later that summer, and nine months later, he would smoke the field at Augusta by twelve shots to win his first Masters title. He would win sixty-four times on the PGA Tour between 1996 and 2008 until a knee injury and his house of cards came tumbling down.

The choices around the gospel of Jesus Christ are actually quite simple. Either you have truly believed that Christ died for your sins, prompting repentance and trust in Christ as your Savior, or you don't. There are only two choices, one for Christ and the other against Christ. Everyone will finish in first or second place at the end of his or her life.

If you know Jesus, you finish in first place. First place is eternal crystal rivers and streets paved with gold. No Jesus means second place. Second place is the eternal inescapable abyss of unending pain and suffering as you look up at the people in first place that you will never speak to again.

As I created this devotion, news broke across the world of the death of Osama bin Laden. Chants of "USA! USA!" erupted from the fans at Citizens Bank Park in Philadelphia, and an impromptu celebration broke out at Ground Zero. Our Wednesday noonday Bible study discussed if Christians should or should not celebrate his death. Certainly, there was no easy answer, given the intense hurt inflicted by this man. However, after almost ten years of "being in first place" and avoiding prosecution, Osama met his untimely match and plummeted to the eternal cellar. During his fifty-four years on earth, given his knowledge of Islam and his intense study of a predominantly Western society, I believe Osama was exposed along the way to the Gospel and the teachings of Christ. He made his choice. Second place.

Prayer: Most holy and just God, I believe that you are perfectly just, and I will determine if I finish first or second eternally. For my friends that I perceive are currently in second place, move my heart to share the Gospel with a sense of urgency and in a loving way. In Jesus's name, amen.

GOLF 76

Hogan's 1-Iron

Psalm 139, 2 Corinthians 5:17, Hebrews 13:5

I will praise You, for I am fearfully and wonderfully made.

—Psalm 139:14

I was on business in New Jersey and had a couple of free hours before dinner, so I drove to the USGA Museum in Far Hills, New Jersey. What an amazing place with so many historical golf artifacts, pieces of memorabilia, and books. I wished that I could get snowed in there for a weekend!

As I came around a corner, there was Ben Hogan's 1-iron enclosed in a glass case! Sure enough, there was a worn spot about the size of a quarter in the middle of the clubface, just as I had heard.

This 1-iron is significant because Hogan used it to strike a memorable shot on the seventy-second hole of the 1950 US Open at Merion Golf Club in Philadelphia. He made an amazing comeback even to play golf again after a horrific car accident in February 1949. Hogan came to the final hole tied for the lead at the end of a grueling thirty-six-hole final that had taken its toll on his weary and painful legs. His tee shot was 220 yards from the green, and he needed a par to force a playoff. Hogan struck a perfect 1-iron to the middle of the green as the gallery collectively gasped at the beauty of the shot played with the most difficult club in the bag. He got down in 2 putts and won the US Open in a playoff the following day.

The 1-iron shot is memorable because of the black-and-white photo that was taken from behind Hogan. His balance is perfect as he poses at the top of his follow-through. Hundreds of people are seen lining each side of the fairway and several thousand encircle the back of the eighteenth green. The photo remains one of the most instantly recognizable pictures in golf history.

The amazing story behind Hogan's 1-iron is that the club disappeared for many years. The 1-iron was discovered in a used club barrel at a pro shop. Apparently someone saw the club and thought, *Only Hogan could have worn that spot in the face of a 1-iron.* Upon further inspection, the club was determined to be authentic and found its resting place in the USGA Museum. How incredible that a club of such value and significance would have been found in the midst of used clubs with very little value and subsequently restored to prominence.

Perhaps you feel like one of the used clubs in the barrel. Society has given you message after message that you are no longer of great value. Perhaps you feel unwanted. You've just been beaten down by the lies of the enemy, job layoffs, sickness, bad financial decisions, misfortune, illness, divorce, peer pressure, rejection, or financial pressure. Your self-esteem has been worn down and you feel that you aren't worth much.

Be comforted that God still believes you are of infinite value. The psalmist assures you that you are fearfully and wonderfully made and that God knew you long before he made you in the womb. God considers you to be so valuable that even if you were the only person on earth, he would have allowed Jesus to be crucified so that you could spend eternity with him. Our God is the God of second chances, and he will never leave you nor forsake you (Hebrews 13:5). God will never stop tracking down his lost sheep.

More than anything, he wants a personal relationship with you through his Son, Jesus Christ. That relationship requires repentance in godly sorrow of any sins that have separated you from God. You must believe and receive. If you truly believe that Christ died for your sins, you can receive Christ as your Savior and Lord, and God will give you a new life. "When someone becomes a Christian, he becomes a new person inside; he is not the same anymore, a new life has begun" (2 Corinthians 5:17 TLB). Won't you give him your life as he reminds you that you are of great value to him?

Prayer: Most holy God, I praise you that no matter how badly I may have failed in my eyes, you still love me the same, unconditionally and infinitely. I am so grateful that you are and always will be there for me. In Jesus's name, amen.

GOLF 77

Be Patient in Trouble

Romans 12:12, 1 Thessalonians 5:17

Be patient in trouble and prayerful always.

—Romans 12:12 (TLB)

One mistake that blows up a round of golf is when a golfer gambles by trying to hit a shot out of trouble that he cannot consistently execute. Suppose that you drive your ball into the woods. There is a narrow opening with out of bounds to the right, but you've got an easy pitch to the fairway to the left. You can gamble and thread the needle or chip out, play for your bogey, and move on. Instead, you try to thread the needle, hit the tree, and the ball goes out of bounds! Before you know it, you've made triple bogey. Still steaming, you gamble on the next tee with the driver to make up for your mistake and drive it into more trouble. Your round is toast, and you're steaming as you toss your clubs in the trunk of your car!

When we get into a spot of bother in our daily lives, we need to be patient. Take the extra time to talk with God and ask him what you should do. To ignore God is to gamble that your emotionally charged decision is not going to be as good as what he would help you decide. Cut your losses by relying on God, going to him in prayer to help with any decision that you need to make, large or small.

Prayer: Most gracious God, so often I get ahead of myself and way ahead of you. May I walk in your footsteps, which will give me the patience to follow your plan, not mine, and make wiser decisions. In Jesus's name, amen.

GOLF 78

My First Glass Smash

The Holy Spirit of God, by whom you were sealed
for the day of redemption.

—Ephesians 4:30

At our 2011 Golf for His Glory Tournament, the golfers were entertained with a Glass Smash competition. Every golfer who bought our event package received two chances to hit a ball through a twenty-four-inch square pane of glass about twenty-five yards away. Five golfers succeeded and qualified for a chance to putt for ten thousand dollars!

What was cool was that when someone smashed the glass, the sound reverberated, and everybody instantly knew that someone had connected! I asked one golfer who broke the glass to describe the sensation. He said, "When I hit the shot, before I could even look up, I heard the sound!" It was the blink of an eye from the time that the ball was struck and subsequently struck the glass!

Once, I "smashed the glass" when I was ten. I had a bad temper without Jesus Christ in my life, and I was frustrated while playing my homemade golf course in my backyard. I chili-dipped one too many shots, and I swung in frustration at the ball. To my horror, it took off on a beeline! The ball skipped off the street in front of my house and crashed into the bedroom window of our neighbor, Mrs. Silas. I panicked, dropped the club, and dashed into the house. I distinctly remember that the phone rang as my foot hit the top step of the porch! My dad drove to the hardware store fifteen miles away, bought a new pane of glass, and replaced my neighbor's window.

With respect to your salvation, it can happen in the blink of an eye. When God senses that you have truly repented of your sins and you have asked Christ to come into your life—*boom!*—it happens just like that. You may not realize exactly when it happened, but several weeks later you will notice that things that seemed so important are no longer important. Eternal disciplines such as prayer, Bible study, and worship take on added importance daily. As quickly as the ball strikes the glass, your life can be changed in Christ, in the blink of an eye.

Prayer: Wonderful Savior and Counselor, thank you for going to the cross and for your free gift of salvation available to me just as quickly as the ball leaves the clubface. It was in the blink of an eye that I was changed forever. In your precious name, Jesus, amen.

GOLF 79

Hit Down to Make the Ball Go Up

Psalm 18:1–2, Matthew 5:1–12, Isaiah 53:5

And by His wounds, we are healed.

—Isaiah 53:5 (TLB)

Golf is seemingly full of contradictions. Perhaps that is one reason the game is so difficult. To make the ball go up, you hit the ball with a descending blow. Beginners try to lift the ball into the air, but that's a sure way to hit a bullet or top the ball. Another contradiction is swinging your hardest does not guarantee that the ball will go farther. It's almost a certainty that the ball will go shorter than a well-timed swing, and it will be more offline. The last one is the explosion from the bunker. Strike the sand two inches behind the ball, never touch the ball, and the ball will plop onto the green? Talk about a shot that requires faith in the mass of tiny particles of matter! But sure enough, by controlling the length of the swing and the amount of sand that you displace, the ball will finish consistently near the flagstick.

The Bible is seemingly full of contradictions. Take the Beatitudes for instance. The secular world teaches us that it's all about power, monetary wealth, and domination, but

Matthew 5 promises that the meek will inherit the earth. And the poor will be rich? What is that all about? The poor have no power, according to the ways of the world. "When I am weak, then I am strong." Huh? When Isaiah prophesied the death of Jesus on the cross, he said, "And by his wounds, we are healed" (Isaiah 53:5 TLB). How can someone's wounds heal our wounds?

Certainly, we don't fully understand the power of God. We must have faith in God that if we live righteously through our Lord and Savior Jesus Christ, we will receive riches that cannot be matched by any financial good fortune. The Bible teaches that the humble and the meek will be exalted. Psalm 73 teaches us that the rich who don't know Christ are undoubtedly on the wrong road. If we can remain faithful, God will bless us now and for eternity. When we don't feel that we can keep going, we can rely on God to give us strength that will carry us through any situation (see Psalm 18:1–2).

Most of all, the blood of Jesus Christ cleanses us from all sin, and the power of his blood covers all of the hurts that have been brought our way.

Prayer: Dear Lord, thank you for the Beatitudes that you shared with us on this earth. The world is so at odds with your teachings. Help me have the fortitude and presence to demonstrate your healing power that is unleashed through humility, kindness, brotherly love, and respect. In your precious name, Jesus, amen.

GOLF 80

Lights, Camera, Action

2 Timothy 4:2, 5

Preach the word of God urgently at all times,
whenever you get the chance.

—2 Timothy 4:2 (TLB)

Our Golf for His Glory Tournament was blessed and honored to have Larry Nelson speak at our prayer breakfast in 2011. Larry is a member of the World Golf Hall of Fame and a three-time major championship winner. We were fortunate to have Larry speak in the year of the thirtieth anniversary of his first major win at the nearby Atlanta Athletic Club in 1981. The PGA of America sent a film crew to capture footage that was aired by CBS the week of the 2011 PGA Championship.

With the camera rolling that morning, Larry had two choices when he spoke to us. He could have played it safe and spoken only about golf or Christ in general. Instead, he told us about his faith and how because he played late on Sunday at the 1981 PGA Championship, he was able to attend his local church that morning. Larry told us that the service calmed him down when the congregation sang

"Victory in Jesus" and "The Old Rugged Cross." He was reminded that no matter what happened that afternoon, he knew that he had already won the eternal victory through his faith in Jesus Christ. He challenged the one hundred golfers and volunteers in attendance to search their hearts for the presence of Christ.

If you had a choice to speak for Christ and share your testimony with the cameras rolling, what would you say? Would you play it safe as the secular world prefers, or would you boldly share your faith as Larry did? Be prepared to "preach the word urgently at all times" (2 Timothy 4:2), "do the work of an evangelist" (2 Timothy 4:5) and share what Christ is doing in your life!

Prayer: Father God, thank you for the courage of the athletes and coaches who take a firm stand for you on and off the playing field, the court, and the golf course. In the holy name of our Savior Jesus Christ, amen.

GOLF 81

"Rors" Like a Lion

Psalm 51:1–10, Romans 7:18–19, 1 Peter 5:8–10

My sin is ever before me.

—Psalm 51:3

The world of golf celebrated the brilliant play of twenty-two-year-old Irishman Rory "Rors" McIlroy, who dismantled the strongest field of the year at the 2011 US Open played just outside the nation's capital at Congressional Country Club. Rory played almost perfect golf for seventy-two holes and broke the Open scoring record by four shots with a scintillating 16-under total of 268. He was serenaded on the back nine with a Big East basketball style cheer of "Let's go, Ror-ee!" His bushy hairdo, his boyish, upbeat personality, the confident hop in his stride, and his stellar performance endeared him to Open fans all week. But it was this startling performance on the heels of his 2011 Masters back nine disaster, when he shot forty-three and blew a four-stroke lead in the final round, that caused golf fans to cheer the loudest. On Sunday night, many people believed that they had just seen the next golf superstar that comes along once a decade.

Rors set a US Open record for most greens in regulation (sixty-one), and his ball-striking was unparalleled in Open history. The only flaw that surfaced in his game was a tendency to hit pull hooks, which meant that occasionally his tee shots would finish in the heavy rough well left of the fairway or green. On Friday, he made double bogey on eighteen after pulling his drive left and hooking his approach shot into the water left of the green.

No matter how good the best players in golf history have been, they have all fought a fundamental flaw in their games. For some players, it's a bad temper (Jones), putting (Watson), chipping (Nicklaus), hooked tee shots (Hogan and McIlroy), blocked tee shots (Woods), or sliced tee shots (Mickelson). For others it has been the mental side of the game (Norman and Weiskopf).

Each person has at least one primary flaw or sin such as pride, anger, greed, lust, or judging others that he or she constantly fights. Satan prowls like a lion (1 Peter 5:8), and he constantly roars at us, especially during our weakest moments. No matter how well things are going, our ugly self will pop up from time to time, even when we just sensed that we were close to God. King David acknowledged in Psalm 51:3, "For I know my transgressions, and my sin is ever before me." Paul penned in Romans 7:18–19, "And I know that nothing good lives in me, that is, in my sinful nature. I want to do what is right, but I can't. I want to do what is good, but I don't. I don't want to do what is wrong, but I do it anyway."

No matter how much Rory practices to keep from hitting a pull hook, he is destined to do it again, and sometimes it will happen at the worst possible moment. The same thing is true with sinful flaws. But you can keep the monster in check by striving daily to be obedient to the Lord through prayer, Bible study, and being accountable to other Christians. Know your limitations, and when the evil one applies the pressure, ask the Lord to help you resist him (1 Peter 5:9) and to strengthen and settle you (1 Peter 5:10). Because you know it's coming sooner or later! Righteousness comes only through Jesus Christ, not from anything you can ever do. When you do slip up, ask God for forgiveness and pray, "Create in me a clean heart, O God, and renew a right spirit within me (Psalm 51:10)."

Prayer: Father God, when I fall short and make a double bogey, please forgive me and assure me that you are the God of perfect love, forgiveness, and the giver of more second chances than I can ever deserve. In the precious name of our Savior and Lord Jesus Christ, amen.

GOLF 82

It's Simply a Matter of Time

Matthew 24, John 2:4, Revelation 19

My time has not yet come.

—John 2:4

Lexi Thompson won the 2011 Navistar LPGA Classic at age sixteen and became the youngest player at that time to win a sanctioned LPGA event. Having qualified for the US Open and US Women's Amateur at the age of twelve, Lexi was already well-known in the world of golf. Earlier in 2011, she had threatened to win the US Women's Open but faded on the last day. She blew up in the final round and finished well behind. Her time had not yet come.

But it was only a matter of time before Lexi Thompson won a tournament. Lexi is almost six feet tall and very strong, hitting her tee shots thirty or forty yards farther than many players. She is very adept with her short irons and an excellent putter. She handles herself on the course with a maturity beyond her teenage years. With her talent and determination, all who follow golf knew it was simply a matter of time before Lexi achieved her first victory on tour.

It's also a matter of time before Jesus achieves his ultimate victory on earth. Having risen from the grave on the third day to fulfill the last of a long list of prophecies, there is one left to be fulfilled. That one will occur when Jesus walks this earth again and wins the Battle of Armageddon and establishes his reign on earth (see Revelation 19). This event is known as the Second Coming of Christ, and many believers are convinced that it will occur. Jesus outlined the events that will occur at the beginning of the end times. There will be wars and rumors of wars and an increase in natural disasters. I googled for "increase in natural disasters" such as killer tornadoes, earthquakes, and tsunamis over the past twenty to thirty years, and dozens of articles and supporting charts appeared. When I googled "decrease in natural disasters," no matches appeared. If it is current evidence that you seek to support the predictions in the Bible, it's there in black and white. It's a matter of time. It's not if Jesus will return, but simply when.

Prayer: Oh Lord, you sent Jesus to us the first time at the perfect time. He will come for the second time in your perfect timing. Help me be ready because I believe that it is just a matter of time. In Jesus's name, amen.

GOLF 83

Pick Me Up, Partner

Ecclesiastes 4:1–10

Two are better than one because they have a good
reward for their labor. For if they fall, one will lift
up his companion but woe to him who is alone
when he falls for he has no one to help him up.

—Ecclesiastes 4:9–10

The Ryder Cup and the President's Cup are two events that
differ from PGA Tour events because they give two golf-
ers who typically compete against each other the oppor-
tunity to compete as teammates. The partner formats are
called best-ball and alternate shot. In best-ball, each player
plays the entire hole, and the better score counts for the
team score. In alternate shot, player A tees off and player B
plays the next shot, and they alternate shots until the ball
is holed.

Alternate shot is tougher because there is the added
pressure of hitting a shot that puts your partner in a pre-
dicament. When one player plays an excellent shot to the
green, it allows the partner to make a less pressure-filled
putt. When one player makes a bad shot, his partner is

there to pick him up. "Pick me up, partner" is often said by one partner to another when he has played a shot that has placed the team in a precarious position. The partner focuses even harder to play a good shot so that his partner doesn't feel bad, and the shoe could be on the other foot on the next hole.

Having a strong Christian partner, whether it is a good friend, a youth pastor, a sibling, or a spouse, makes it easier to live daily as a Christian. When you are faced with a difficult shot in life, you can consult your Christian partner and receive godly advice and counsel for how to overcome the difficulty. It relieves the pressure when someone gives you good advice, encourages you, and prays for you. Always remember that you inherited a partner for eternity, the Holy Spirit, when you received Christ. How comforting it is that the Holy Spirit is always there to help you! Be still and listen for his guidance.

Prayer: Father God, help me remember that I am never alone when I choose to confide in a brother or sister in Christ or simply in the Holy Spirit whenever I need help. In Jesus's name, Amen.

GOLF 84

You're Always Enough for Me

Psalm 63

In a dry and weary land where there is no water.

—Psalm 63:1

For five years, our church, Mt. Zion UMC in Marietta, Georgia, hosted Golf for His Glory, a golf event that raised funds for MUST Ministries and sought to glorify God as an outreach vehicle to bring men and women closer to Christ. One unique feature was a "tee box" testimony placard that was placed on each tee box with scripture and insight into the faith journey of a well-known athlete or coach.

We were honored in 2010 to have a Mt. Zion member, US Senator Johnny Isakson, speak at our prayer breakfast. Johnny shared a story that occurred when he was a teenager on a mission trip in Mexico. Johnny told us that the event remains the most touching witness for Christ that he had experienced.

At the evening church service, Johnny and his friend were sitting on the next to last pew. A young mother came in with her baby and sat down in the last pew. Her clothes were dirty, and she was obviously poor. In a thoughtful gesture, Johnny's friend retrieved several pesos from his pocket. He wrapped the peso bills around a card with a drawing of Jesus and handed them to the young mother. She thanked the boy for his gesture and handed the pesos back to Johnny's friend. But she kept the drawing of her Savior. Despite her economic poverty, this woman was obviously rich in a way that many will sadly never experience. Why was she rich? Because Jesus was always enough for her.

She would surely appreciate the lyrics from the Casting Crowns song, "Always Enough," two generations later. Mark Hall (of Casting Crowns) remembered: "Several months ago, we lost a soldier in Afghanistan who was part of our church. His son is in our middle school ministry, and it really rocked us. You know it's going on, but then it happens close to you, and it opens your eyes to the reality. Casting Crowns was on the road and couldn't be home for the funeral. The song really came together that day. When life is hard and tragedy comes, you discover how real Jesus is to you. Your friends and your church try to help, but at that moment, Jesus can't be Plan B. He's got to be it; He's got to be enough. When things that are constants in our lives are stripped away, that's when we have to know He's 'Always Enough.'"

This devotion is a tribute to our Mt. Zion mission teams who minister in Costa Rica and Brazil. May many hearts be transformed through these people who seem to have so little, yet have so much of what we all need, which is simply Jesus. Because Jesus is always enough for you and me.

Prayer: Most Holy God, I yearn for the strong faith of that young mother in Mexico. No matter what my circumstances are or what life throws at me, may Jesus always be enough for me. In the precious name of our Savior, amen.

GOLF 85

Jimmy, Do You Play Golf?

Isaiah 64:4, 1 Corinthians 2:9

Eye has not seen, nor ear heard, nor have entered
into the heart of man, the things which God has
prepared for those who love him.

—1 Corinthians 2:9

For five years, I served as a marshal at the PGA Tour
Championship at East Lake Golf Club. Once, I was posi-
tioned to the left of the eighteenth green near the player's
walkway to the scorer's tent. Darren Clarke, winner of
the 2011 Open Championship at Royal St. George's in
Sandwich, England, came off the course and was very dis-
appointed in his driving of the golf ball.

A ten-year-old boy named Jimmy was the sign boy for
Darren's group. In his Ulsterman Northern Ireland lilt,
Darren called out, "Jimmy, do you play golf?" Jimmy didn't
answer. Either he didn't hear Darren, or he was too startled
to respond.

Darren persisted, "Jimmy, do you play golf?"

This time, Jimmy responded with several rapid nods.
"Yes, I do play golf!"

Clarke reached into his golf bag, pulled out the TaylorMade R7 driver that had given him fits, and handed it to the shocked young boy. Jimmy walked away with a huge grin on his face.

Later that afternoon as I sat on one of the shuttle buses that would take us back to the Turner Field parking lot, Jimmy proudly walked onto the bus carrying the R7 driver, which was almost as long as Jimmy was tall. He sat down in front of me.

I said, "Are you going to give that driver to your dad?"

Jimmy shook his head firmly and said, "No, this is mine!"

When Jimmy came to the course that day, he could not have dreamed that he would be leaving with a club that was used by a golfer in the tournament. Jimmy's sudden good fortune reminded me how God's surprises are like the sun breaking through on a cloudy day. They come when we least expect them, and no way can we predict what they will be. If we stay obedient, God has great surprises in store for us.

Prayer: Father God, thank you for the blessings that seem so routine that I sometimes take them for granted. May I appreciate them just as much as the bolts out of the blue that you love to use to surprise your faithful children. May the smile on my face pay you sufficient homage. In Jesus's name, amen.

GOLF 86

Comeback at Sandy Run

Hebrews 11:1–6

What is faith? It is the confident assurance that
something you want is going to happen.

—Hebrews 11:1 (TLB)

Following college, my brother LE taught school in Warner
Robins, Georgia. He joined Sandy Run Golf Club and
played golf almost daily in the summertime. I would visit
him and play golf for three or four days in a row. There was
a youth golf tournament at Sandy Run, and I signed up to
play in the thirteen- to fourteen-year-old division.

I was so nervous on the first tee! The first hole was a long
par four, and I topped my tee shot, which went about forty
yards. I topped my second shot and wound up making a nine!
I settled down and played bogey golf until I got to the fifteenth
hole. On fifteen, I made a sharp-breaking six-footer for a par.
Pumped up, I walked to the sixteenth tee where I had the
honor. I hit a 6-iron in the middle of the green and walked off
the tee with a strong sense of satisfaction and self-confidence.

But Mr. Arnold Smith, our scorer and referee, called
me over. I would find out years later that his mother was

a wonderful woman and big Braves fan who lived next to Becca's Uncle Donald in Livingston, Tennessee. Mr. Smith said reluctantly, "Danny, I'm sorry, but you teed off outside the markers. I must assess you a two-stroke penalty."

The tee box was wide, and all week we had played from the right side of the tee. But the tee markers had been moved to the left side! My heart sank and I teared up. I two-putted for my five. Now I trailed my friend Tommy Wood by one shot. But I made two six-foot par putts on the last two holes and won by a shot! I still have the trophy at home, and I got my picture in the Warner Robins newspaper!

What was the lesson that I learned? Keep fighting through disappointment, even when all seems lost. Don't give up. God never gave up on you. Ever. No matter what you've done or what you're going through, there is always hope in Christ for a victorious life. Christ loves us so much that he never gave up on the cross.

Prayer: Lord, help me keep the faith when I fall behind or the ball bounces the wrong way on the field or in life because you never gave up. You never gave up at Calvary, and you never gave up on me and never will. Thank you for your incredible love, which I do not deserve. In the strong grip of the Savior, amen.

GOLF 87

Losing Our Preshot Routine

2 Timothy 3:16, 1 Thessalonians 5:17

Pray without ceasing.

—1 Thessalonians 5:17

I played in the 1978 Wallace Adams Memorial Tournament at Little Ocmulgee Golf Club in McRae, Georgia. After the first day, I was tied for the lead in the first flight, which is the flight just below championship. With another good round, I could win my flight and receive two hundred in golf merchandise, so I was motivated to play well.

I was on fire on the front nine. I shot a two under par thirty-four and hit all nine greens in regulation. My longest birdie attempt was twenty feet, so thirty-four was the worst that I could have shot. Everything was clicking, and I made four pars on ten through thirteen. However, I began to hit the approach shots farther and farther from the hole, and I had to work hard to save my par on thirteen with a long two-putt from seventy-five feet.

But I unraveled after popping up my tee shot on four-teen. I made bogey followed by three more bogeys and a disastrous double-bogey on eighteen that took me out of the running. I was so aggravated at myself! Looking back, I discovered the root cause of my downfall. As the pressure mounted, I began to take too much time over the ball. My arms tightened, and my rhythmic front-nine swing became herky-jerky on the back nine. To be a consistent golfer, it is important to have a consistent preshot routine, which means to take your setup position, look at your target, waggle, look again, waggle, and swing. I saw a Golf Channel program where pro golfer Denis Watson demonstrated his preshot routine, and it was fourteen seconds every time he did it.

Let's examine the spiritual routines in our daily lives. Just as daily physical workouts strengthen our bodies, daily spiritual disciplines (e.g., prayer, Bible reading, fellowship with other Christians) develop your heart. Tony Eubanks, a Clemson University football team chaplain, once told me about the spiritual two-a-days that his players observed. Their two-a-days consisted of morning devotions and evening Bible reading with ample prayer time.

When we skip our daily Bible reading or go longer between prayers or miss a couple of Sundays of church or Bible study, it throws us off our game. We will be less consistent and exhibit less fruit of the Spirit (Galatians 5:22–23). We start making bogeys by being irritable or lustful or envious when normally that would not be our pattern. We become less obedient, and thus we're less productive for the kingdom. Let's stick to our daily spiritual disciplines, and we will make more consistently good shots for God!

Prayer: Most gracious Father, help me avoid the tug of the evil one who wants to take me out of my routine. Help me be strong in you because you and I are always stronger than the evil one. In Jesus's name, amen.

GOLF 88

Trunk Slamming

Matthew 13:42–50

There will be wailing and gnashing of teeth.

—Matthew 13:42

Saturday is called moving day on the PGA Tour as golfers vie to get into contention for Sunday's final round. It's the day to move up the leaderboard. However, the golfer must first deal with Friday, which is called cut day. Golfers must make the top sixty so that they can play two more days to try to win the tournament or at least have a high finish.

For those who miss the cut, Friday is also trunk slamming day. A tee shot in the water, a misplayed approach, or a three-putt on eighteen are all ways to blow the chance to play on the weekend. When the golfer gets to his courtesy car and thinks about the mistakes he made and the money he squandered, *wham!* There is the unmistakable slam of the trunk. It's no money earned and bye-bye until the next tournament.

I think of a dividing line between spiritual and material blessings. Spiritual blessings include trust, integrity, honesty, love, peace, joy, and salvation. None of these items can be purchased, and they rise above the line, pointing toward heaven. Material blessings are nice, but they fall below the line. If those become our focal points, greed will be our driving force, and we miss the cut. All of the fame and fortune in the world won't save us from God's judgment.

The love of money, which turns into greed; the love of power, which turns into selfishness; and the love of fame, which chokes out humility, will ultimately lead to disillusionment, dissatisfaction, and disaster. There has never been one joyful person in hell, which means there is a lot of trunk slamming after the ultimate missed cut, which is missing the final opportunity to repent from sin and receive Christ.

Prayer: Father God, I don't want to be a trunk slammer when it comes to missing out on your kingdom. Please forgive my sin and give me the joy and peace that only comes from knowing the Savior of the world, Jesus Christ. In Christ's precious name, amen.

VERSES BY BOOK

1 Corinthians	
2:9	Golf 85
6:18–20	Golf 51
9:22	Golf 30
1 John	
1:9	Golf 03, Golf 22, Golf 66
1 Peter	
5:7	Golf 38, Golf 65
5:8–10	Golf 81
1 Samuel	
12:1–12	Golf 08
1 Thessalonians	
5:11	Golf 63
5:17	Golf 77, Golf 87
2 Corinthians	
5:17	Golf 06, Golf 21, Golf 76

2 Peter	
2:9	Golf 24
2 Timothy	
2:19	Golf 62
3:16	Golf 29, Golf 50, Golf 87
3:16–17	Golf 69, Golf 74
4:2	Golf 33, Golf 34, Golf 80
4:5	Golf 80
4:7	Golf 12
Acts	
1:8	Golf 32, Golf 37, Golf 41
20:24	Golf 30, Golf 70
Colossians	
3:17	Golf 01
Ecclesiastes	
4:1–10	Golf 83
Ephesians	
2:8	Golf 22
2:8–9	Golf 37
4:30	Golf 32, Golf 78
5:20	Golf 18

6:10	Golf 32
Exodus	
20:1–19	Golf 27
20:7	Golf 49
Galatians	
5:22–23	Golf 56
Hebrews	
10:17	Golf 20
10:30–31	Golf 75
11:1–6	Golf 57, Golf 86
13:5	Golf 76
Isaiah	
40:22	Golf 53
40:25–26	Golf 53
50:7	Golf 07
53	Golf 60
53:1	Golf 26
53:4	Golf 39
53:5	Golf 11, Golf 79
64:4	Golf 85

James	
4:7	Golf 51
4:8	Golf 25
Jeremiah	
6:16	Golf 05
29:11	Golf 22
29:13	Golf 19
John	
2:4	Golf 82
3:16	Golf 15, Golf 22
3:16–17	Golf 06, Golf 48
3:30	Golf 53
8:7	Golf 36
8:32	Golf 03
11:25–26	Golf 14
14:6	Golf 02, Golf 43, Golf 45
15:5	Golf 10
Jonah	
3	Golf 23
Joshua	
1:8	Golf 47

Lamentations	
3:22–23	Golf 28
Luke	
9:62	Golf 30
17:3–4	Golf 36
18:1	Golf 59
24:49	Golf 67
Mark	
5:37	Golf 44
14:33	Golf 44
Matthew	
5:1–12	Golf 79
5:27–32	Golf 54
6:9–13	Golf 64
6:33	Golf 58
7:7	Golf 31
7:13	Golf 02
10:32–33	Golf 45
13:36–50	Golf 55
13:42	Golf 75
13:42–50	Golf 88

17:1–2	Golf 44
18:22	Golf 36
24	Golf 82
25:32	Golf 02
26:34–49	Golf 46
28:1–6	Golf 72
28:1–9	Golf 06
Philippians	
1:6	Golf 61
4:6	Golf 59
4:13	Golf 01, Golf 68
Proverbs	
3:5–6	Golf 52, Golf 71
27:17	Golf 04
Psalms	
7:11–13	Golf 24
18:1–2	Golf 79
51:1–10	Golf 81
51:4	Golf 08
63	Golf 84
73	Golf 75

119:100–109	Golf 29
119:105	Golf 05, Golf 58
139	Golf 76
139:14	Golf 22
150	Golf 73
Revelation	
19	Golf 82
Romans	
2:1–16	Golf 24
5:8	Golf 13, Golf 22, Golf 42
6:23	Golf 09
7:7–9	Golf 40
7:18–19	Golf 54, Golf 81
8:1	Golf 20
8:26	Golf 23, Golf 32, Golf 41, Golf 71
8:28	Golf 58, Golf 70, Golf 71
10:13	Golf 35
12:1–2	Golf 61
12:10	Golf 63
12:12	Golf 17, Golf 59, Golf 77

INDEX

Churchill, Winston	Golf 18
Cink, Stewart	Golf 15
Clampett, Bobby	Golf 70
Clarke, Darren	Golf 85
Couples, Fred	Golf 31
courage	Golf 06, Golf 14
Crane, Ben	Golf 63
Crenshaw, Ben	Golf 32, Golf 37
D	
daily discipline	Golf 46, Golf 47
Davis, Brian	Golf 52
De Vicenzo, Roberto	Golf 27
determination	Golf 28, Golf 29
Drum, Bob	Golf 48
E	
Edwards, Bruce	Golf 28
Elkington, Steve	Golf 29
Els, Ernie	Golf 70
encouraging fellow believers	Golf 63
F	
faith	Golf 12, Golf 37, Golf 57
faith, sharing your	Golf 80
fear, overcoming	Golf 68
forgiveness	Golf 20, Golf 36

Fowler, Rickie	Golf 63
Furyk, Jim	Golf 52, Golf 59
G	
Gans, Danny	Golf 21
Giglio, Louie	Golf 53
God, child of	Golf 10, Golf 22
God, give the glory to	Golf 73
God, gives the increase	Golf 53
God, including	Golf 41
God, love of	Golf 09, Golf 12, Golf 15, Golf 30, Golf 32, Golf 42, Golf 60
God, relationship with	Golf 25
God, surprises from	Golf 85
God, values people infinitely	Golf 76
God. watching over us	Golf 65
God's plan	Golf 58
God's power	Golf 67
grace, under pressure	Golf 17
gratitude	Golf 21
Grout, Jack	Golf 64
H	
Hall, Mark	Golf 84
Harmon, Claude	Golf 34

Jesus Christ, resurrection of	Golf 72
Jesus Christ, second coming of	Golf 82
Jesus Christ, wounds of	Golf 79
Johnson, Dustin	Golf 29
Johnson, Zach	Golf 04, Golf 11, Golf 29
Jones, Bobby	Golf 22, Golf 27, Golf 55
Judgment Day	Golf 24
K	
Kaymer, Martin	Golf 29, Golf 57
Keeler, O. B.	Golf 22
Kite, Tom	Golf 32, Golf 72
L	
Langer, Bernhard	Golf 09, Golf 57
legacy	Golf 12, Golf 13
Lehman, Tom	Golf 16
Leonard, Justin	Golf 37
light unto my path	Golf 05
Lord's Prayer	Golf 64
love (see God, love of)	
Lundquist, Vern	Golf 05, Golf 34, Golf 72
lust	Golf 08
M	
Mackay, Bones	Golf 71
Maravich, Pete	Golf 80

Maria-Olazabal, Jose	Golf 57
Marr, Dave	Golf 33
McCollister, Tom	Golf 48
McDowell, Graeme	Golf 59
McIlroy, Rory	Golf 29, Golf 58, Golf 81
McKay, Jim	Golf 26
mercies, new each day	Golf 28
Mickelson, Phil	Golf 45, Golf 53, Golf 55, Golf 58, Golf 66, Golf 71
Mize, Larry	Golf 04, Golf 10, Golf 62, Golf 73
Moody, Larry	Golf 10, Golf 11, Golf 14
N	
Nakajima, Tommy	Golf 55
Nelson, Larry	Golf 13, Golf 80
Nicklaus, Jack	Golf 07, Golf 05, Golf 28, Golf 29, Golf 31, Golf 34, Golf 44, Golf 48, Golf 55, Golf 58, Golf 64, Golf 67, Golf 72
Nordeman, Nichole	Golf 60
Norman, Greg	Golf 73
O	
obedience, striving for	Golf 81
O'Grady, Mac	Golf 68

P	
Palmer, Arnold	Golf 33, Golf 44, Golf 46, Golf 48, Golf 58, Golf 59
passion	Golf 33
patience	Golf 77
peace	Golf 11, Golf 12
Penick, Harvey	Golf 32
Perry, Kenny	Golf 17, Golf 36
perseverance	Golf 05, Golf 19
Player, Gary	Golf 18, Golf 44, Golf 58
prayer	Golf 18, Golf 28, Golf 59
prophecy	Golf 26
R	
repentance	Golf 08, Golf 22, Golf 40, Golf 43
Richt, Mark	Golf 04, Golf 65
S	
salvation	Golf 02, Golf 08, Golf 13, Golf 22, Golf 42
sanctification	Golf 61
scripture, guidance from	Golf 69
scripture, study of	Golf 74
sharing Jesus Christ with others	Golf 20

Weiskopf, Tom	Golf 34
White, Slugger	Golf 52
Wind, Herbert Warren	Golf 46
Woods, Tiger	Golf 08, Golf 11, Golf 24, Golf 36, Golf 49, Golf 58, Golf 75
Z	
zeal	Golf 30, Golf 33

REFERENCES

Golf 01 Alex and Stephen Kendrick, writers. *Facing the Giants the Movie.* Directed by Alex Kendrick. 2006.

Golf 02 Hepp, Michel. *Golf Digest*, 2005.

Golf 06 Wikipedia.com. "Ben Hogan."

Golf 08 Bright, Bill, executive producer. Jim Green, executive director. *Jesus.* 1979.

Golf 09 Langer, Bernhard. "Reborn." Links Players International, 2007.

Golf 10 Mize, Larry. "Significance." Links Players International, 2007.

Golf 11 Stricklin, Art. "After Winning the Masters, Johnson Credits the Master." BPSports.Net, April 18, 2007.

Golf 12 Stewart, Tracey with Ken Abraham. Taken from *Payne Stewart: The Authorized Biography.* Hopeway.com. Christian Ditchfield. Anastasia T. Stewart. Used by permission of Broadman & Holman Publishers. 2000.

Golf 13 Harris, J. Gerald. "Georgia Baptist golfer Nelson to be inducted into World Golf Hall of Fame." *The Christian Index*, October 26, 2006.

Golf 14 Russell, Robert. Taken from *Zinger*. www.preach-him.org/Christiandeath.htm. "Resurrection Promises." *Preaching Today*, May 9, 2008.

Golf 15 Harris, J. Gerald. "Stewart Cink: Premier Golfer, Christian Gentleman, Missionary Volunteer." *The Christian Index*, 2005.

Golf 16 Lehman, Tom. "I Felt Like a Failure." Links Players International, 2007.

Golf 17 "The 2009 Masters Golf Tournament." Masters.org, April 13, 2009.

Golf 17 "Kenny Perry's Old Kentucky Home–3 Tours & News." http://www.golf.com/golf/tours_news/article/0.28136,1839965–3.00.html.

Golf 18 "Ron Green Jr." Charlotteobserver.com, April 11, 2009.

Golf 19 Jasper, Kelly. "Broadcaster Pat Summerall Shares Faith at Masters Breakfast." *The Augusta Chronicle*, April 7, 2009.

Golf 27 *What a Day, What a Masters*. Doug Roberson and Furman Bisher. *AJC*, April 12, 2009.

Golf 27 "Bobby Jones." http://en.wikipedia.org/wiki/Bobby_Jones_(golfer).

Golf 33 http://findarticles.com/p/articles/mi_m0HFI/is_4_54/ ai_100839553/.

Golf 34 Kelley, Brent. "Did Ben Hogan Really Fail to Notice an Ace?" *Brent's Golf Blog*, October 26, 2011.

http://golf.about.com/b/2010/10/26/did-ben-hogan-really-fail-to-notice-an-ace.htm.

Golf 34 CBS Masters Telecast. April 13, 1986.

Golf 37 Lagarde, Dave. "Crenshaw Is a Firm Believer in Fate." September 10, 2008. http://www.pgatour.com/2008/tournaments/r060/09/10/award_2/index.html.

Golf 43 "Sport: Lee Trevino: Cantinflas of the Country Clubs," *Time Magazine*, Monday, July 19, 1971.http://www.time.com/time/magazine/article/0,9171,905380-2,00.html.

Golf 45 Augusta National Information–Masters Tournament Info.http://www.mastersgolftickets.com/augusta_national.html.

Golf 46 Wind, Herbert Warren. "Let Us Now Praise Amen Corner." *Golf Digest*, April 1984.

Golf 48 Huber, Jim. "Good-bye to One of Golf's Best Friends." March 2, 1999. http://si.cnn.com.

Golf 48 "1960 US Open at Cherry Hills." http://www.arnoldpalmer.com/experience/exhibits/1960_usopen_cherryhills.aspx.

Golf 56 Bacon, Shane. "When Losing a Golf Tournament Really Makes You a Winner." May 7, 2010. http://yahoo.com.

Golf 59 Facey, David. "Hail-in-One, Webb's Prayers Are Answered." June 19, 2012. http://www.thesun.co.uk/sol/homepage/sport/golf/4379678/Webb-Simpson-wins-US-Open.html.

Golf 64 http://www.worldprayers.org/archive/prayers/invocations/our_father_which_art.html, The Lord's Prayer–Matthew 6:9–13.

Golf 84 Hall, Mark. "Always Enough." 2009.